THE STATION NOW STANDING

By the same author

Promenades and Pierrots
By Royal Command
Dad's Army: The Making of a Television Legend

British Library Cataloguing in Publication Data
Pertwee, Bill
    The station now standing: Britain's colourful railway
    stations.
    1. Great Britain. Railways. Stations
    I. Title

    ISBN 0-340-54685-9

Published by Hodder and Stoughton,
a division of Hodder and Stoughton Ltd,
Mill Road, Dunton Green, Sevenoaks, Kent TN13 2YA
Editorial Office: 47 Bedford Square, London WC1B 3DP

Designed by Trevor Spooner
Maps drawn by Alec Spark

Photoset by Rowland Phototypesetting Ltd, Suffolk
Printed in Great Britain by
Butler and Tanner Ltd, Frome and London

The publishers would like to thank Gordon Biddle for supplying the historical text.

The author and publishers would like to thank the following for supplying photographs on the pages indicated:

R. Bamberough, pages 57 (left), 98–99; John Barnes, page 3; British Rail, pages 5, 15, 17 (bottom), 55 and 93; British Rail
Eastern Region Photographic Unit, pages 21 and 31; Bruce's Brewery, page 88; Colin Byrne, page 53; Brian Chambers,
page 48; Lionel Jeffreys, page 39; Ian Dean, pages 83, 85 and 86; Direct Image Design Ltd, page 57 (right); John East, page
61; John Goss, page 67; Great Western Society, Didcot, page 124; Walter Harris, pages 122–123; Ian Macdonald, page 70;
Austin Maher, page 23; the keeper of The National Railway Museum, York, pages 9, 25, 41, 57 and 75; M. Newman, page 19;
David Perry, Community British Rail Unit, pages 10, 12, 17 (top), 45 (bottom), 55, 76, 90, 104 and 119; The Railway
Heritage Trust, pages 68, 73 and 87; John Sagar, pages 14, 29, 35, 37 and 71; ScotRail, page 11; Steam Photography, page 69.

Unacknowledged photographs have been taken by the author.

The publishers have tried to contact all copyright holders but where inadvertent infringement has been made they apologise
and will be happy to make due acknowledgment in all future editions.

THE STATION NOW STANDING

BRITAIN'S COLOURFUL RAILWAY STATIONS

BILL PERTWEE

Hodder & Stoughton
LONDON SYDNEY AUCKLAND TORONTO

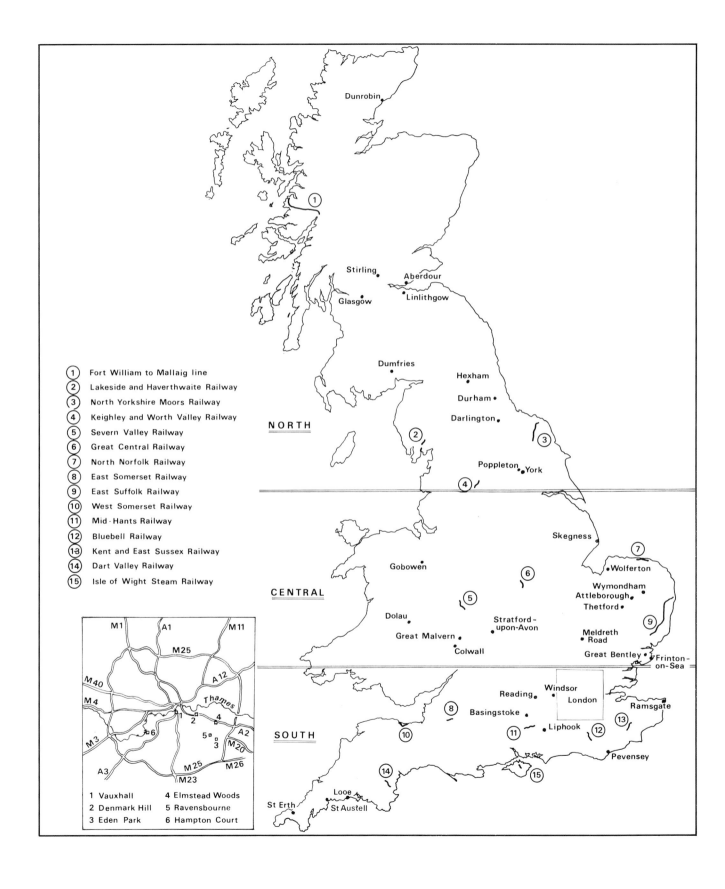

1 Fort William to Mallaig line
2 Lakeside and Haverthwaite Railway
3 North Yorkshire Moors Railway
4 Keighley and Worth Valley Railway
5 Severn Valley Railway
6 Great Central Railway
7 North Norfolk Railway
8 East Somerset Railway
9 East Suffolk Railway
10 West Somerset Railway
11 Mid-Hants Railway
12 Bluebell Railway
13 Kent and East Sussex Railway
14 Dart Valley Railway
15 Isle of Wight Steam Railway

NORTH

CENTRAL

SOUTH

Dunrobin

Stirling
Aberdour
Glasgow
Linlithgow

Dumfries

Hexham
Durham
Darlington

Poppleton York

Skegness

Gobowen
Wolferton
Wymondham
Attleborough
Thetford

Dolau
Stratford-upon-Avon
Great Malvern
Colwall
Meldreth Road
Great Bentley
Frinton-on-Sea

Reading
Windsor
London
Basingstoke
Liphook
Ramsgate
Pevensey
St Erth
Looe
St Austell

M1 A1 M11
M25
M40 A12
M4
Thames
M3 A2
M20
A3 M25 M26
M23

1 Vauxhall   4 Elmstead Woods
2 Denmark Hill   5 Ravensbourne
3 Eden Park   6 Hampton Court

CONTENTS

Acknowledgments 6
Introduction 8

ACKNOWLEDGMENTS

I realised when I started this book that, apart from being a regular traveller, I knew very little about the railway system and its stations in this country. I hope it is not too immodest to say that since then I have learned a lot, but there is still much more to discover. It has been an enjoyable experience and I have met many interesting and helpful people in the process. Research for any subject has to have a starting point, and the reaction of the person or persons you meet at that point have a great influence on the overall project.

My first contact for this book was the photographic section of the architectural department of British Rail at Croydon and the very enthusiastic Paul Childs. Paul then recommended that I see Leslie Soane, a director of the Railway Heritage Trust. Leslie and his assistants John and Sarah have been very helpful, on more than one occasion may I add, in lending me pictures and transparencies. I am also very grateful to the Hon. Sir William McAlpine, Chairman of the Trust, for his contribution to the text concerning the Trust's activities.

Leslie Soane introduced me to David Perry, the Partnership Manager of British Rail's Community Unit. The first time I met David I realised at once what a very knowledgeable person he is on all aspects of the railway, and his kindness in giving me of his time and advice and lending me many photographs and transparencies have been of great assistance. Gordon Biddle's contribution to the station histories has been really invaluable and I am most grateful to him.

I owe extreme gratitude to the British Rail Community Unit and individual members of staff throughout BR for their kind co-operation.

As far as the Preserved Railways are concerned, Walter Harris of the West Somerset Railway showed immediate willingness to help, and so did John Sagar of the Keighley and Worth Valley Railway who with his superb photography made my research very much easier in this area of the railways.

Roger Stubbs of the Severn Valley Railway gave me his valuable time, and pictures, as did Ian Dean, the Managing Director of the Mid-Hants line.

David Madden of the North Norfolk, my friend David Shepherd the artist and Don Sartin of the East Somerset Railway took time out to help me, which I appreciate.

Klaus Marx, Bernard Holden, Mr Bamberough of the Bluebell Railway have helped, so too has John East of the Great Central Railway who showed me round the very interesting Loughborough Junction.

John Mann, who not only serves the Dart Valley Railway Company but also manages the Company's unique cinema.

I am also indebted to photographer Roger Penny at Paignton, Mike Murfin of the Kent and East Sussex Railway, and also Hal Dyer for her local history details.

Terry Hastings of the Isle of Wight Railway, Moira Russell of the North Yorkshire Moors Railway, and Austin Maher of the Lakeside and Haverthwaite Railway have all been most helpful.

Very early in my search for attractive stations I met David Turner at Wymondham in Norfolk. He has been a great inspiration to me and I am sure to railway enthusiasts in general.

C. J. Wignall's wonderful book *British Railways Maps Gazetteer* has been a constant help in my research of past and present stations.

I must also thank Gordon Smith, the ScotRail photographer, for his help, so too David Thompson, Sue Wells and Steve Fountain in the Public Affairs Department of British Rail Eastern Region Headquarters in York, Graham Warner, the Manager of British Rail's Poppleton Nurseries and Gary Smith at

Waterloo. I was delighted too to meet Margaret and Douglas Fuller at their Meldreth Road Crossing House and to receive their unstinted hospitality.

I was delighted with the memories my actor friend Bernard Cribbins was able to recall of *The Railway Children*. Actor/Director of the film Lionel Jeffries had nothing to contribute because all we did was laugh on the telephone, which is what we do (in all the wrong places) when working together, but he readily sent me a picture from the movie. Mrs Opie of Woodbridge in Suffolk was most helpful, and Mrs Connie Fairey took a lot of trouble in furnishing me with details of Colwall.

I do hope I shall be able to spend a little more time with Roger Hedley-Walker and his wife at the lovely Wolferton Station Museum when I am next in the area.

Peter Howard's contribution will be most informative to readers I am sure.

Jeanette Howse and Charles Whetmath at the Great Western Society, Didcot, thank you.

Jonathan Barker in Cornwall was a great help in taking photos of St Austell for me after my camera had gone on the blink. Jean Sanderson of the Frinton and Walton Heritage Trust, John O'Connor at Ramsgate, John Watling and his details of Great Bentley Station, Alex Metcalf for his contribution on Brunel; all your help is much appreciated.

Thanks are also due to the Basingstoke and Dean Borough Council's publicity department and the libraries of Cornwall, Bromley and Horsley.

My wife Marion has been most patient during the writing of this book, but has threatened never to go near a railway station again! Nevertheless she has been a great help with research.

Last but not least what would I do without Geraldine Guthrie. Geraldine deciphers my scribble, somehow seems to make sense out of it, and eventually serves up beautifully typed pages of text. I have decided that if Geraldine retires from secretarial work I will retire from writing.

If I have forgotten anyone please forgive me, I certainly didn't mean to.

Thanks to you all.

INTRODUCTION

In the course of compiling this book I have travelled hundreds of miles up and down the country visiting many railway stations, some large, some not so large, country halts and several preserved lines in search of station buildings with a colourful flavour and a general air of cleanliness and pleasing architectural design. To see a restored station that once suffered years of neglect gives a great feeling of satisfaction in the knowledge that people do care about the railways. Who would have thought a few years ago that you would enjoy waiting on the concourse at Glasgow Central, or on the platforms at Wakefield and Chesterfield, all of them in the heart of industrial or thickly populated areas of commerce?

I have talked to the staff on small stations who for years have cared for their working environment, and made it as pleasing as possible to the eye of the traveller and I have encountered many associations or groups of individuals within the community who have taken it upon themselves to enhance the well being of 'their' station. I've met eccentrics (thank goodness there are a few left in the country), railway enthusiasts whose interests probably go back to their childhood and railway staff who have given up much of their spare time to see that their stations are well cared for, and in many cases, with their interest in gardening, a feast of colour. Some businesses have leased station buildings from British Rail and while spending money and time on their upkeep have turned the interiors into many varied uses. A few stations have been bought as private homes but are still used by travellers.

British Rail are putting their financial resources into new track and rolling-stock, which is certainly badly needed in some areas, but they also have some resources to spend on redecoration and refurbishment of stations small and large, and this refurbishment will I am sure grow. I do think it is important to look after those stations which were built with care and artistry, to serve not only the traveller but also to give pleasure to the eye. Much has already been achieved in some areas by British Rail and the Railway Heritage Trust in conjunction with local communities

to make travelling as pleasant as possible, sometimes in very difficult circumstances and without the essential ingredient, money. Don't forget few other national railways are required to meet break-even financial targets.

The preserved railway companies also deserve praise in continuing to enhance station environments. Apart from the refurbishment of railway architectural heritage the displays of flowering shrubs, bedding plants and window boxes are on view in both large and small stations. Sadly in a few cases environmental achievements have been spoiled, and personally I think the reason for this is because staff at some stations are only on official duty for a few hours a day. Staff are the authority required to keep a station safe from vandalism and free from the littermongers who now seem to be part of our everyday lives, but that's another problem. I would also add that unmanned stations may deter potential community involvement, which is where their assistance can be invaluable. Perhaps one of these days we'll have a few station masters back on the railway – wouldn't it be a good move? and to complete the well-being of our communities why don't we have the policeman back on the beat and matrons back in hospitals.

I think in the main it is difficult for the younger generation coming into the railway business to have the enthusiasm and desire to look after their stations as the more senior staff have done for years. The youngsters have many distractions nowadays and the money to pay for those distractions, so maybe this is understandable. When today's old guard (no pun intended) retire, local communities must look around them and see how they can help and perhaps educate some of the youngsters in the art of growing flowers and other little chores that have given some of our stations a pleasing atmosphere.

If you are near one of the stations mentioned in the following pages, pop in and see the staff and give them a pat on the back, or leave a note for whoever is responsible from the local community if they are involved, they'll appreciate it.

Rotten Row 1895   A.K.Zinkeisen

LONDON by L·N·E·R
IT'S QUICKER BY RAIL
FULL INFORMATION FROM L·N·E·R OFFICES AND AGENCIES

ABERDOUR
Opened 1890
North British Railway
Listed Grade B

The railway came late to Aberdour; until the Forth Bridge was built the nearest station was the Forth ferry terminal at Burntisland, some two and a half miles away, but on the opening of the connecting line the village was given a station of its own.

In earlier years the style might well have been influenced by the 14th century Aberdour Castle nearby, but by 1890 the railways were less indulgent to such flourishes, particularly the North British which had thirty-five per cent of the cost of the new bridge to pay for, not to mention a number of expensive new lines leading to it. Even so, Aberdour was given better buildings than at other small stations on the new line at Dalmeny and North Queensferry, which were built of wood. The sturdy stone structures, despite being built in a style common on many railways at that time, were no doubt intended to reflect the growing popularity of the village as a residential and holiday watering place, and remain substantially unaltered today.

ABERDOUR

Someone said to me 'You don't go to Aberdour Station to catch a train, you go to spend some time in a miniature Kew Gardens.' This may be a slight exaggeration, but never-the-less you almost feel it a shame when your train arrives and you have to leave the amazing display of flowers and shrubs that appear in every shape and form and in every type of container throughout the station. Special occasions, such as a Royal Wedding, are commemorated with unusual and artistic floral displays in the platform beds. Even the waiting-room and entrance to the booking-hall are decorated with flowers, and if you want to read the latest garden magazines they are available in the carpeted (yes carpeted!) waiting area. The quite amazing appearance of this now well-known ScotRail station is all due to one man and, I'm sure he would agree, in no small measure to his wife. Andrew and Gwen Philip have created all this in their spare time, growing the plants from seed and seeing them through all weathers into fruition. Friends' greenhouses were used at one time, but British Rail have now provided the Philips with two of their own. The station has won many awards in various competitions as you can imagine, including the 1990 Best Kept Station Award, and long may it continue. It is wonderful when people care about their working surroundings and at the same time bring joy to other people. An example to us all.

The Philip's pride and joy

DUNROBIN

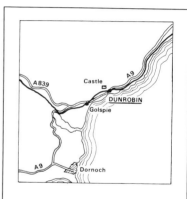

If you travel on British Rail's Inverness to Thurso and Wick line in the north-east of Scotland you will be travelling over a part of railway history. The section between Golspie and Helmsdale was built by the Third Duke of Sutherland. That was in the days when various railway companies operated throughout the country until the big four took over in 1923. The Duke of Sutherland's home was Dunrobin Castle, situated on his vast estates. He not only owned the stretch of line but also Dunrobin Station and his own engine and saloon coach which he was allowed to run between Inverness and Wick, and to Kyle of Lochalsh.

The station is between Golspie and Helmsdale and in recent years has been repaired and repainted. British Rail trains occasionally stop at the station to enable tourist parties to visit the castle. The Duke's tank engine was called *Dunrobin* which was kept in a shed at Brora and his private saloon was kept in a shed next to Dunrobin Station. His son, the Fourth Duke, replaced the tank engine *Dunrobin* with a larger engine for which a new shed was built at Golspie. The Fourth Duke often liked to drive the engine himself and had a special leather-cushioned seat fitted across the back of the cab for himself and his friends. The Duke was a Director of the Highland Railway, and it was his habit to travel to board meetings at Inverness in style in his own saloon coach.

Incidentally the Third Duke's first wife (presumably the Fourth Duke's mother) was the Countess of Cromarty, a rather eccentric lady and a religious fanatic, who spent most of her time living in two rooms in her London home Stafford House (now an art gallery), lying on a sofa covered with a red silk eiderdown and surrounded by parrots and mynah birds, her only food a diet of chicken. All very eccentric!

The restored Dunrobin Station

11

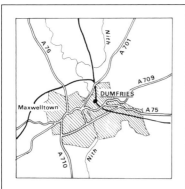

DUMFRIES
Built 1859
Glasgow & South Western Railway
Listed Grade B

The first railway through Dumfries was the Glasgow Dumfries & Carlisle, opened in 1848. After it became the Glasgow & South Western in 1850 a new station was built in red sandstone, fairly plain but sturdy, in true Scots fashion. The most impressive parts of the station are the elaborate glass-and-iron platform awnings which were probably added around the end of the 19th century. The frontage is enlivened by delightfully frilly valancing along the eaves of the roofs and around one of the dormer windows.

As late as 1979 a notice on the road bridge at the end of the down platform warned enginemen that 'Emission of smoke likely to cause a nuisance is strictly prohibited', eleven years after steam had disappeared on British Rail.

DUMFRIES

Dumfries stands on the River Nith, in Border country to the south-west of Glasgow, and boasts five bridges which are steeped in history. One of its claims to fame is that Robbie Burns, the great Scottish poet, wrote 'Auld Lang Syne' here and he is buried in St Michael's churchyard in the town. I hope he saw the New Year in first!

A FAVOURITE RAILWAY JOURNEY
The Railroad to the Isles
by John Sagar

The railway map of Britain contains many majestic stretches of line. One thinks, for example, of the run along the sea wall at Dawlish, the magnificent stretch of the east coast mainline north of Berwick-upon-Tweed, or virtually the whole of the Settle and Carlisle line, that splendid tribute to vaulting Victorian ambition. If forced to choose one route which stands out from all the rest, however, I would turn not to one of these great mainlines, but to something altogether more humble and remote; the Fort William to Mallaig Extension of the West Highland Railway.

Lest the observer should think that this single track, steeply graded line with its many speed restrictions and fluctuating seasonal traffic is a poor relation of high-speed routes further south, it should be remembered that it was one of the most expensive lines to build in Britain. Traversing frequently inhospitable territory between the shores of Loch Linnhe and the Sound of Sleat, the Mallaig line is of particular note, in that it saw the use of mass concrete as a building medium on a hitherto unprecedented scale. The head of the firm of contractors appointed to construct the line, Robert McAlpine, was affectionately known as 'Concrete Bob' in civil-engineering circles. The twenty-one concrete arches of the graceful Glenfinnan viaduct, described by the Scottish writer J. J. Bell as 'a thing so delicate that the fairies might have built it', stand as an enduring monument to his pioneering work. Opened on 1st April 1901, the Mallaig line permitted the West Highland Railway to tap the fishing industry and Hebridean traffic, which was already starting to contain a fair amount of tourism. This it has continued to do in varying degrees for its owners ever since.

The Beeching Report, published in 1963, proposed the withdrawal of the passenger service from the Mallaig line. This would have been a tragic step for, although such an argument is likely to cut no ice with an accountant, it must be said that the greatest appeal of this railway lies in its romantic historical associations and the sheer magnificence of its setting. ScotRail even provides us with a regular steam-hauled service in the summer months, with which to savour the line even more. This thoughtful flourish and the introduction of fast, efficient 'Sprinter' diesel trains, has also made this 'railroad to the isles' more financially secure.

One of the finest views to be enjoyed from the train between Fort William and Mallaig is from Glenfinnan viaduct to the celebrated monument to Bonnie Prince Charlie, standing proudly and defiantly at the head of Loch Shiel. The historian will have a further poignant reminder of what the '45' meant to the Highlands as the train passes Loch Nan Uamh and the place where Prince Charles Stuart landed in July 1745.

The scenic splendours of this line are almost too numerous to catalogue and what is also remarkable is that the Mallaig line loses none of its appeal when it is raining, and the quiet water courses are suddenly transformed into raging torrents. It is no wonder that men who have driven trains over this stretch for forty years or more say they are still not bored with it.

The Mallaig Extension, a long way from HQ, also retains endearing human qualities. For instance, it is not uncommon to see trains making unscheduled stops between stations to save passengers a long walk home in the wet! Such a civilised approach to life is doubtless fostered by the splendour to which train crews are constantly exposed: be it the view of a snow-capped Ben Nevis from the shores of Loch Eil, the dramatic steep climb away from Glenfinnan, the mountains mirrored in the tranquil waters of Loch Eilt, the lonely little chapel high up at Polnish Bridge, or the island chain of Much, Eigg, Rhum and Skye glimpsed across the silver sands of Morar.

Rationalisation has taken its toll of stations on this line and today several boast only a rudimentary 'bus shelter'. However, at Arisaig and Glenfinnan, one can still see examples of the celebrated West Highland chalet-style building, now painted white and two-tone green, which is striking if nothing else. A society has even been set up to preserve Glenfinnan as a complete, working West Highland railway station. Let us hope that its customers, as they sit in their mountain fastness, will be disturbed by the sound of passing trains for generations to come!

John Sagar is a member of the Keighley and Worth Valley Railway Preservation Society, and the Editor of their magazine *Push and Pull*.

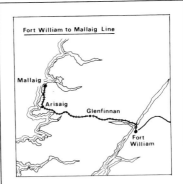

Glenfinnan Station

FORT WILLIAM TO MALLAIG LINE

'Fort William to Mallaig', the title alone has a romantic and slightly mysterious sound about it, and this line is certainly for the romantics. As John Sagar has pointed out, there is more dramatic scenery on this line than on any stretch of railway in the British Isles.

One of the features of the line is the recent establishment of a museum and museum trust at Glenfinnan Station which records the history of this branch line. The Station Museum Trust is a private project developed by Mr John Barnes who lives nearby although ScotRail/British Rail are co-operating with the Trust, so that this typical country station will continue to be used for the general travelling public.

Restoration work is presently taking place on part of the signal-box which is being refurbished as a reading-room and reference library and will give visitors a chance to find out about the whole area surrounding the West Highland Railway, and of course the stations themselves. A picnic area is also being developed at Glenfinnan with viewing points and nature trails for tourists. Apart from the station being a listed building, which makes the whole project of refurbishment so worthwhile, it must help travellers to enjoy this area of Scotland even more. Think of it, you can get on a train in London and with just two changes you can be in the beautiful Isle of Skye via Mallaig.

Another feature of Glenfinnan is the accommodation. John Barnes has refurbished the station cottage, which originally housed the station-master and this is now available for hire as a holiday cottage. It has all mod cons and can sleep up to six people. What a lovely spot to use as a base for discovering all the wonders of this line. You may like to stay and spend some of your time helping the Museum Trust with some of the work that has still to be done at the station complex. John Barnes would be delighted if you did, and details of the facilities you can expect at the cottage can be obtained from him at Station Cottage, Glenfinnan, Inverness-shire PH37 4LT. Or you might just like to become a friend of the Museum Trust, annual membership is so very little, and they would be most grateful for your help. Best of all, see it all for yourself – go on treat yourself!

GLASGOW

Glasgow's Central is now one of the most prestigious stations in Britain. The whole centre of the building has been redesigned and it is certainly worthy of the city which recently achieved the title of 'the cultural city of Europe'. It is Scotland's largest city, and with its deep waters of the Clyde originally developed into a centre for heavy industries and ship-building during the industrial revolution. The famous ocean liners *Queen Mary* and *Queen Elizabeth* were launched there.

The cultural side of the city is certainly well-established with its fine King's Theatre, concert halls, orchestras, and as the home of the Scottish Opera. Two of the most famous football teams in the land, Rangers and Celtic still battle it out on the green turf of Ibrox Park just as they have done for many years. The late comedian Will Fyfe's famous song 'I belong to Glasgow', or the mention of Sauchiehall Street and its pubs, is certain to bring a tear to a Scotsman's eye, or on the odd occasion a rise in his blood pressure and the use of fisticuffs.

I have had some great times in Glasgow, including seeing the now obsolete trams tearing along the main thoroughfare ringing their bells furiously to avoid the crowds.

GLASGOW CENTRAL
Built 1879–1907
Caledonian Railway
Listed Grade B

The station complex falls into a number of chronological parts. The earliest is the main entrance in Gordon Street and the heavy trussed roof covering the concourse and the inner ends of platforms 1–8, which dates from 1879–82, although the concourse then was very much smaller. Platform 9 was added in 1889. Under a huge enlargement programme of 1899–1905 the original platforms were lengthened outwards to the Clyde Bridge, which itself was duplicated, and platforms 10–13 were built on the west side, all under a much lighter trussed roof with delicately curved lower members. The architect for the original station and the massive Central Station Hotel (1883) was Sir Robert Rowand Anderson, while James Miller was responsible for the architecture of the station extensions, a 1907 extension to the hotel and the Union Street office block of 1901. Miller also designed the Argyle Street bridge.

But the main credit for the station we see today goes to the Caledonian's engineer-in-chief, Donald Mathieson, who created the broad, uncluttered concourse that now house shops, restaurants and sales kiosks, that have been retained in ScotRail's recent and admirable restoration scheme.

15

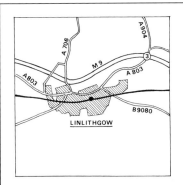

LINLITHGOW
Built 1842
Edinburgh & Glasgow
Railway
Listed Grade B

Among the few remaining original stations on the Edinburgh & Glasgow, Linlithgow has the best-preserved building, especially since its sympathetic restoration, to which the modern, curved, glass-topped waiting shelter on the opposite platform acts as a splendid foil. The station entrance is tucked away in a sidestreet at the foot of a high-walled embankment which contains the entrance stairs and subway. The up side awning, now cut back, on attractively painted iron columns and intricate brackets was probably added by the North British Railway later in the last century.

If you are travelling around Scotland by train you could start your sightseeing in the best way, at Linlithgow Station. Halfway between Edinburgh and Glasgow, Linlithgow is a peaceful town with many wonderful old buildings which will certainly please any intended visitor. The town is also steeped in history.

James I of Scotland built a palace here in 1424, on the site of an earlier one destroyed by fire and Mary Queen of Scots was born in the castle in December 1542, the ruins of which are now designated an ancient monument. In the church of St Michael you can see a bell reputed to be at least five hundred years old, that was tolled after the Scottish defeat by the English on the field of Flodden.

STIRLING

Stirling Station is clean, the staff are courteous, and it appears to have displays of brightly coloured plants almost everywhere. It is used by many thousands of visitors each year, particularly by those who wish to see the castle.

When I visited the castle it was a beautiful day, so the view from the battlements was very impressive. I couldn't help thinking though how daunting it might look from a distance, to an army advancing in misty weather. The castle, dating back to Alexander I in the twelfth century, is on the crowning point of a massive rock formation overlooking the Carse of Forth, and the town has grown up around it. James V of Scotland was born at Stirling Castle and his daughter Mary, the future Mary Queen of Scots, lived there during her childhood. Her son, the future James VI of Scotland and James I of England (he united the thrones) had a son Henry who was born at the castle, and baptised in the Castle Chapel Royal in 1594. They were not the luckiest of families; Mary Queen of Scots was beheaded, her grandson Henry, James's eldest son, died in his youth, and Henry's younger brother Charles I who succeeded to the throne lost his head in Whitehall in London.

Within the precincts of this fine building is a magnificent regimental museum which is extremely informative in its history of Scottish Regiments and their service worldwide.

Before I filled my 'head' with any more history from the Stirling guide-book I went back to the station to bring me back to the future and have another look at the flowers and drink a cup of tea.

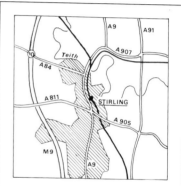

STIRLING
Built 1912
Caledonian Railway
Listed Grade B

In railway terms Stirling Station is relatively modern. Designed by James Miller, who we have already met at Glasgow Central, it replaced a much older station built for the Scottish Central Railway by the noted Perth architect Andrew Heiton in 1848. The modest stone façade is enlivened by typically Scottish crow-stepped gables, the Scottish lion and the railway company's initials and date. The chief glory is inside, where the concourse surrounding an unusual circular ticket-office is covered by a curved, glass roof that describes striking geometrical patterns, repeating on a smaller scale a similar theme by the same architect at Wemyss Bay nine years earlier.

The station still has semaphore signals, although they are likely to be replaced by colour lights before long, and Stirling Middle signal-box just south of the station is now the largest remaining mechanical signal-box in Scotland.

The eye-catching flowers on top of John Menzies' bookstore and the unusual architecture make Stirling a very attractive station

DARLINGTON
Built 1887
North Eastern Railway
Listed Grade II

In 1849 Queen Victoria criticised Darlington Station for its shabby appearance, but despite the royal displeasure the North Eastern Railway did nothing about it until 1887, when William Bell, the company's architect from 1877 to 1914, rebuilt it with a triple-arched roof characteristic of his work.

Known as Darlington Bank Top from about 1870 to 1934, the present station is basically formed by a long, broad island platform with all the offices and passenger accommodation ranged down the middle. There is a sloping road approach from the bridge at the north end and a second entrance facing the town, with a subway leading to the platform. This entrance, in red brick with Dutch gables, incorporates a strikingly tall clock tower which, at the top of the hill, is one of the main landmarks of Darlington. It was attractively restored and floodlit in 1990, with substantial aid from the Railway Heritage Trust.

Darlington's other station, North Road, which dates from 1842 and is on the pioneer Stockton & Darlington Railway. The first station of 1825, an attractive Georgian-styled building with a wooden-roofed train-shed, now houses an excellent railway museum and is scheduled as an Ancient Monument.

DARLINGTON

Everyone who lived in, or close to, Darlington in the heyday of steam-engines was in some way connected with the railways. The town is synonymous with George Stephenson, the early pioneer of steam, just as Brunel is associated with the Great Western Railway in the south-west. It must have been a shock to the town when the hustle and bustle of the steam and steel suddenly stopped. I've been told that the atmosphere in pubs, clubs and shops that were once alive with chatter was one of shock and subdued conversation, and in some places silence.

The people of the north-east are some of the friendliest folk in the country, and when I visited the town for the first time to work in the theatre there, the people's resilience shone through as new small industries were beginning to emerge and laughter and purpose was brought into their lives once more. I've found the Civic Theatre in Darlington (originally the Hippodrome) one of the happiest places to work in, and on a Saturday between the matinée and evening performances the theatre club supporters lay on a delicious spread of goodies for the actors. I have stood many times on historic Darlington Station when changing trains for nearby Billingham and I have tried to imagine that first journey of Stephenson's steam *Rocket* from Stockton to Darlington.

The restored station clock

DURHAM

One of the stops on the journey from London to Edinburgh is Durham. When I stopped there on my fairly recent journey to Scotland I didn't have much time to take any pictures, but I was amazed at the amount of flower troughs and hanging baskets that were displayed in this station.

I think it is only right that travellers should be greeted in this way, particularly those who are heading into this city to discover all the marvellous historical places of interest that it has to offer. The beautiful Norman cathedral dominates the city from its position high up on its rock, surrounded on three sides by the River Wear. The cathedral became a shrine to St Cuthbert and his tomb can still be seen there, along with that of the Venerable Bede. Durham Castle (built in 1070) and the University form part of the old city which offers many more historical delights.

Durham is also famous for its Miners' Gala when miners from all over the country congregate every year in July to celebrate with music and comradeship.

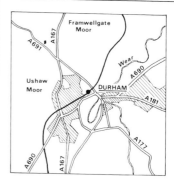

DURHAM
Opened 1857
North Eastern Railway
Listed Grade II

The station sits at the end of a viaduct looking out across the Wear to Durham Castle and the cathedral. It is appropriately built in stone in a Tudor style, with tall, coupled chimney stacks, mullioned windows and a crenellated Gothic-arched entrance. With the matching station-master's house adjacent they formed an imposing pair of buildings well in keeping with the ancient city they served. Deep, broad awnings, probably added in 1870, gave ample protection to the platforms. Recent restoration work has removed over a century's accumulation of clutter, although unfortunately the house was demolished some years ago.

HEXHAM

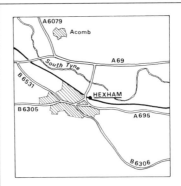

HEXHAM
Opened 1838
Newcastle & Carlisle
Railway
Listed Grade II

Over the years considerable additions and alterations have been made to Hexham Station, tending to hide the original parts. However, the stone screen walls which supported an overall roof still stand at the back of the platforms and the original station house is on the west side of the entrance, connected to the present station building which was built later by the Newcastle & Carlisle's successor, the North Eastern Railway. That company was also responsible for the fine platform canopies which, with the iron footbridge, were typical of that company's designs, although the latter has now lost its glazed sides and roof. The whole station is in the attractive creamy-buff stone of the neighbourhood.

If you are visiting this historical region of the north-west of England your pleasure will hopefully begin at Hexham railway station. Hexham is a beautifully designed building, built before British Rail took it over, but which they have maintained with care, and quite rightly so because the architecture of the canopies alone is really fine when both platforms are in sight. There are plenty of flowers on view to add to the effect and the hanging baskets in particular give the whole station an extra feeling of beauty. No doubt the floral arrangements come from Poppleton nurseries but they are well cared for by the staff at Hexham.

The station has had its share of awards for its appearance, so next time you are alighting from or boarding a train there let the station staff know you appreciate their labours – it doesn't take long and it will certainly please them.

Hexham itself is on the banks of the River Tyne, some twenty miles to the west of Newcastle, and not far from Hadrian's Wall. Three miles away from the city centre lie the ruins of the Roman city of Corstopitum, surrounded now by its modern counterpart in Corbridge. When the Romans finally left Britain Hexham had become fairly important, and in AD 674 Queen Ethelreda gave some land to Bishop Wilfred to found an abbey. Much of the stone used in the building was taken in the good old Anglo-Saxon tradition from the nearby deserted Roman town; it happens nowadays if you leave a row of houses empty for too long. Latin inscriptions to Emperors and Gods can be found on the masonry used in those early rebuilding times and it is interesting to wander around the abbey in search of Roman graffiti.

Bishop Wilfred incidentally spent many years in Selsey, that delightful part of Sussex that was once quite remote and unspoilt, a lot of it still is thank goodness. The Bishop built a church there before going to Hexham and converted many local fishermen to Christianity. They even gave up using bad and crude language for him. 'By jove, I've had a spiffing catch today.' Unlike Hexham where tangible evidence of the Bishop remains, the Sussex church is now under the waves some miles offshore in the English Channel, though many a local resident will tell you that the church bells can be heard ringing on a stormy night. One of the Bishop's fishermen getting his own back perhaps for not allowing him to use the odd swear word.

An interesting find from Hexham, a bronze bucket in which were 8,000 coins of Anglo-Saxon origin, is now in the British Museum. Perhaps the proceeds from one of the Bishop's collecting plates in the abbey.

And so endeth the lesson!

Above: The typical iron footbridge and fine canopies of the North Eastern Railway, viewed from the line

Left: Examples of some of the beautiful plants and baskets supplied by nearby Poppleton Nurseries

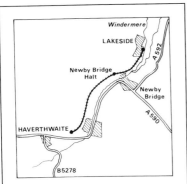

THE LAKESIDE AND HAVERTHWAITE RAILWAY

'This preserved line is part of a branch that was built by the Furness Railway Company for passenger travel and tourism. The Company was originally created during the industrial revolution when it was used to transport iron-ore and coal mined in the north-west of England. As passenger steamers began to use nearby Lake Windermere for the tourist trade it seemed a natural progression for the railway company to become involved. The Furness Company planned the southern end of Lake Windermere as a terminus for their branch line, which would be a direct link with the Barrow-in-Furness mainline to Carlisle and would automatically complement the steamer trade on Windermere. By the 1870s the iron-ore business had begun to dwindle, but in Cumbria the passenger trade was increasing, particularly with the Lakeland tourist resorts.

Once the branch was built the golden years existed until the First World War, but in the 1920s and '30s it failed to regain its popularity, as the motor-car became a serious competitor. Apart from some freight traffic on part of the line and the moving of German prisoners of war in the 1940s business dwindled and closure loomed. This finally occurred in 1967.

It is doubtful whether the preservation of part of the line would ever have happened if it had not been for a local farmer, Charles Maher, who was a keen cine-photographer. Charles and his brother Austin decided to photograph some railway traffic in the area and this sparked off thoughts of the closed Haverthwaite branch. Two of their friends had previously expressed interest in preserving the branch and reopening it as a working line that could once again link up with the steamer trade on Lake Windermere.

It is now history how this was achieved. After several petitions had activated the issue and with the backing of the local MP, the main stumbling block was the Lake District Planning Board, the local authority who advised British Rail, the then owners, that the line should be closed and the track removed. A local authority actually working against local opinion! It was the then Minister of Transport, Mrs Barbara Castle, who eventually saved the day. She decreed that the branch line could not be dismantled without her permission. Isn't it wonderful when the boss steps in and makes a decision and doesn't pass the buck.

Preserved railway societies have had their share of battles with bureaucracy but none more so than the Lakeside and Haverthwaite. The initial action failed but Jim Morris and Austin Maher decided to fight on and try to save the project of the preservation of the branch. The tenacity of Morris and Maher and the new L&HR Co, in spite of opposition from some quarters, eventually achieved their goal. It must have been a wonderful day for them and all the volunteer workers when the line from Haverthwaite to Lakeside was finally opened on 2nd May 1973. The line

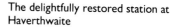

is one of the smaller preserved branches in the country, but has a great variation of scenery along its route.

Haverthwaite Station itself is extremely welcoming and has been refurbished to include some of the original features of the station. Today the restaurant and tea-room is licensed and can be used for special party bookings, and they make a point of welcoming children for educational purposes and tours of the locality.

On leaving Haverthwaite by train you soon pass through some of Cumbria's loveliest scenery. After the Leven Valley and the river below with its waterfall there is a gradual climb for about a mile before going under a hillside bridge and out into forest land and its profusion of grazing deer. At this point you may also see idiotic sheep sometimes holding up the train; they have no respect for timetables! The summit of the line is Newby Bridge Halt and the scenery changes once again, passing behind the Swan Hotel and through woods of fine oak trees and pines and then glimpsing the shores of the southern extremity of Lake Windermere. These shores are full of every kind of wildlife imaginable. Then it is slowly in to Lakeside Station and the landing stage for the steamers.

It is rather a shame that Lakeside Station itself was stripped of a lot of its finery before the company was able to preserve the line, but plans have recently been passed by the Lake District Planning Board so the Windermere Iron Steamboat Company (The Windermere Steamers) can rebuild the Lakeside Station house and offices to their original design and retail outlets built where the original goods warehouse stood.

The view of the lake as you arrive is quite breathtaking and makes you appreciate all the more the efforts of everyone responsible for reopening this branch that gives you so much to look at and enjoy. If you have booked to go out on to Lake Windermere with one of the steamer cruises your pleasure will be even more enhanced, and don't forget you still have the journey back to Haverthwaite to look forward to after your trip.

PRESERVED RAILWAYS

In the early days of the preserved railway companies, around the Beeching era of British Rail closures, much criticism was laid at the door of the enthusiasts who were trying to save or reopen a station or two. Demonstrations (peaceful ones of course) were held outside town halls, and people lobbied their MPs and Parliament. 'Grown Men and Women Playing Trains' was the allegation aimed at them.

If it hadn't been for the small band of eager and determined folk 'playing trains' many thousands of people would have been deprived of the pleasure of seeing what a country station used to look like, and how it was run all those years ago in the heyday of steam. We certainly wouldn't want our national railway system to go back to those rather dirty sooty days of steam, but it is part of our heritage, and these small railway companies have played their part in preserving it. Because of these enthusiasts, millions of youngsters all over the country can now experience the steam age at first hand. Just think, we may never have heard the laughter and excited chatter of children who have experienced a visit to one of the preserved stations. And as the early years of the few grew into thousands, doctors, politicians, clergymen and other professional people have become avid enthusiasts of the preserved railways and lifelong friendships have been forged through these railway preservation societies. For everyone though, the views of stations like Crowcombe and Stogumber on the West Somerset line, the first glimpse of Dartmouth and its spectacular scenery as the train draws into Kingswear on the Paignton and Dartmouth Railway and the beautiful little Staverton Station of that same railway company, all give immense pleasure.

Film companies are also grateful that the early pioneers of the railway preservation societies achieved their aims because nearly all of their stations have been used to great effect by film and television producers for their period productions including *The French Lieutenant's Woman*, *Poirot* and *Campion* and Oakworth on the Keighley and Worth Valley Railway is now famous for its involvement in the filming of *The Railway Children*. Not to mention Arley and Highley on the Severn Valley Railway and Weybourne and Sheringham on the North Norfolk Railway where scenes were shot for the *Dad's Army* television programme 'The Royal Train'. They all have a romantic air about them.

It would take many hours and many more words to relate all the problems and obstacles that had to be overcome by the small groups of people who initially led the way in preserving even just a few miles of railway line, but we can see the success stories in the railway companies that have now grown into flourishing businesses and popular attractions.

NATIONAL RAILWAY MUSEUM YORK

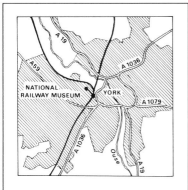

The City of York is renowned for its museums. If you are interested in the history of our railways or just love the sight of the big steam monsters of the past that have hauled our trains all over the country, and not forgetting the modern-day counterparts, then this museum is for you.

This exhibition, because that's what it is, really has everything, and to enjoy it or use it for reference studies you really need to make time to take it all in, and even then my betting is you'll want to go again. It has working signal systems, workshops, a research library, lecture theatre-cum-cinema and shops.

In the Great Railway Show in South Hall, which is a separate building, you can see every conceivable type of engine, with their gleaming brass and original painted liveries of the different railway companies, and cut-out sections of some of the steam and diesel locomotives show just how the power is generated. There are examples of rolling-stock that have been restored to their former glory, grand saloons specially built for royalty, the interiors furnished in splendour beyond belief and which make you realise what craftsmanship was all about a hundred and fifty or more years ago; very ordinary suburban 3rd-class carriages which must have been fairly uncomfortable to travel in; a Southern Railway Electric motor coach and night ferry sleeping car on the London/Paris/Brussels run of the 1930s and the simple but important railway horse-drawn luggage delivery wagon of yesteryear.

All generations are catered for – there are model train layouts for those enthusiasts who have played with a small train set on their living-room floor, plus railway toys of all kinds in a new interactive exhibition called 'Magician's Road', specially designed for young visitors.

You cannot do justice in this short space to the National Railway Museum, but perhaps it has whetted your appetite for a visit if you are in or near York.

A general view of the splendid Great Railway Show

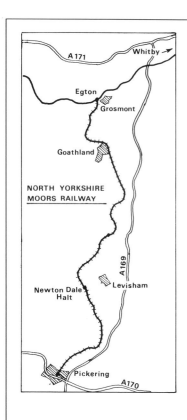

NORTH YORKSHIRE MOORS RAILWAY

Of all the preserved railway lines in the country the North Yorkshire Moors Railway must be one of the most historical, as far as the railways are concerned. The first line of which the North Yorkshire Moors Railway is a descendant was opened between Whitby and Pickering in 1836, but it was a horse- (yes horse) drawn train that made the inaugural journey. This early line across the moors was called the Whitby and Pickering Railway Company, but the journey using horses would have been rather like riding in a stage-coach on rails.

At various points on the line farmers were ready at strategic places with new teams of animals. The changeover by the railway staff was heralded by a white flag or handkerchief being waved from the line. Naturally there were some severe gradients and at the incline at Beck Hole a large rope had to be used for propulsion. Charles Dickens remarked, 'I travelled on a quaint old railway along part of which passengers are hauled by a rope.' As time went on it was obvious that the line had become accident-prone, and just wasn't safe enough. There had been some fatalities and injuries to passengers, and this certainly couldn't continue. Safety measures were put into operation, and the line prospered, but the original company only lasted a few years before wealthy landowner and Railway King, George Hudson, decided to use steam power and replan the route from Whitby as part of his York North Midland Railway.

George Hudson had quite by chance met the Father of the Railways, George Stephenson, at Whitby in Yorkshire in 1836 and they became united by the idea that Yorkshire should have further rail communication. Stephenson had already been the architectural genius behind the Stockton and Darlington and Liverpool Manchester Railways, which had paved the way for countrywide railway expansion, and his meeting with the wealthy Hudson meant it was not long before plans were drawn up for Whitby to have its own railway.

As time went by the moors and coastal lines were again improved and passenger and freight traffic proved a popular source of income. Raw materials brought to Whitby from as far afield as the Baltic could now be moved efficiently with Pickering becoming a busy junction for several lines. In 1914 the double track into Pickering was single tracked for four miles so the rails could be used for the French war effort but unfortunately the ship carrying the rails was torpedoed by the Germans and they now lie at the bottom of the English Channel.

The London and North Eastern Railway took over the area in 1923 and one of their innovations was to run excursions from West Yorkshire towns via Pickering to Scarborough and Whitby with stops for lunch and tea. The moors have always been lovely places to live in but even now some areas are very remote, and in the early days of the railway, communication for the inhabitants was difficult. Many of these folk worked for the railway and an ingenious ploy was used by some of them for posting letters. A slit was made in a willow or hazel branch, the mail was then stuck in it and the branch bent low enough for the train driver or fireman to snatch

the mail from the branch and take it on its way to the nearest posting stage. In the 1960s wholesale closures of lines including the Whitby to Scarborough, Whitby to Redcar and most of the moors' routes were closed. Luckily, along came the North Yorks Moors Preservation Society which preserved one of the lines, and created the North York Moors Railway which is certainly a popular tourist attraction, set in beautiful surroundings, so it is not only the pleasure you have of travelling on a preserved railway but there is the bonus of everything the accompanying countryside has to offer. The first train ran on the reopened line in 1969, but it wasn't until May 1973, after all the usual hard work and negotiations, that the line was officially opened by the Duchess of Kent and she unveiled plaques at Grosmont and Pickering and at the Angel Hotel, Whitby where the historic meeting between George Hudson and George Stephenson took place and the first regular passenger trains went into service. By 1973 the assets of the company had been transferred to a new body with charitable status, the North York Moors Historical Railway Trust. The English Tourist Board had also made a loan to the company because they had realised the potential of the railway as a first-class tourist attraction, and a way to advance the education of the public in the history of rail locomotion in the area and the North York Moors National Park.

If you start your journey at Pickering you have the chance to see the twelfth-century castle, a huge trout farm and the Black Swan Inn where the original opening of the railway was celebrated. Further on, Levisham seems very remote high up on the moor but the station is very traditional in its structure, followed by Newtondale Halt, a request stop which cannot be reached by road, so if you're alighting here make sure you know the time of the last train otherwise you'll have to spend the night on the moor. Between Levisham and Goathland are the three huge radar scanners of the Ballistic Missile early warning system – you can't possibly miss them. The next stop, Goathland, has many interesting features in the town and surrounding walks. There are also hotels and guest-houses nearby and the area is surrounded by heather-laden hills.

And now on to Grosmont which has the locomotive shed and workshops for the line, and plans for further expansion. There is also a pub at Grosmont adjacent to the station. I have not yet had a meal in one of the dining-cars on this line but it is something I'm looking forward to on the 'North Yorkshireman' service. The menus seem very mouthwatering. A typical winter one is:

MENU

Smoked Salmon Mousse
Hor d'oeuvres

Cream of Asparagus Soup
Lobster Bisque

Roast Turkey with all Traditional Trimmings
Roast Sirloin of Beef in Red Wine Sauce

Selection of fresh vegetables

Individual Christmas Pudding with Hot Rum Sauce
Hazelnut Roulade

Cheese and Biscuits

Coffee and Mints

I can't wait. All washed down with a bottle of Château Lafite, but don't tell Mrs Lipton! (BBC television's *You Rang, M'Lord?*).

By the way the North York Moors Railway Trust would be awfully pleased if you joined them.

Goathland Station

I have been very fond of Yorkshire for many years. At the start of my theatrical career I spent a fair amount of time working in the theatres at Leeds and Bradford, and I got to know Yorkshire and its people pretty well. The countryside certainly delighted me and the moors in particular, with their unique atmosphere which can be both stimulating and relaxing. In the areas around Howarth and the Brontë Parsonage you almost feel you can see Heathcliffe running over the surrounding moorland. It is difficult to describe the delights of Ripon and Barnard Castle, with its superb Bowes Museum, the magnificence of the city of York (at times almost brought to a standstill in the tourist season) and the market town of Thirsk with its welcoming inns full of chatter with racing gossip. A little further west is the sleepy village of Dishforth, once alive with airmen during the Second World War. My brother is buried in the RAF cemetery there.

When I have appeared in the theatre at Billingham in Cleveland I have always tried to persuade my fellow actors to spend at least one day visiting the small Yorkshire coastal villages of Staithes, Robin Hood's Bay and the larger fishing port of Whitby, with its superb selection of fish and chips, cooked only as they know how to in Yorkshire and costing only £4.00 with a glass of wine and a goodly slice of newly baked bread and butter. If only the customers of London's over-priced eating houses knew what they were missing!

POPPLETON NURSERIES

One of the unusual aspects of British Rail Eastern Region is Poppleton Nurseries: two acres of glasshouses and seed beds adjacent to the Harrogate/York line, a few miles from the City of York. In 1941 the nursery was converted from Poppleton Station Goods Yard and was taken over by the District Engineer at York who turned it into a garden. They started with one greenhouse and by 1988 have gradually expanded to twelve. The garden originally started to produce trees and shrubs for scenic lineside planting and is now responsible for landscaping, jointly carried out with the Local Planning Authority.

The nurseries are managed by Graham Warner, a friendly fellow with a natural love of the soil, who is very proud of some of the railway stations that have been considerably enhanced with his floral decorations. One idea of Graham's, to ease the movement of bulky materials at the nursery, such as bales of peat, compost, coke for boilers and trays of plants, was the inauguration of its own narrow-gauge railway. A two-foot-gauge track was laid from one end of the garden to the other on which run hand-propelled wagons obtained as scrap from recently closed narrow-gauge internal systems. This is always a very popular attraction at open days held during York Festivals. Nearby is Poppleton Station, a charming building with a glass canopy, comfortable wooden seats and a profusion of flowers. Adjacent to the station are the level-crossing gates and Poppleton signal-box, where you will have to ring if you want to leave a message for Graham. The nurseries have a very good arrangement with the North Yorkshire Moors Preserved Railway whereby they supply flowers to Pickering Station (the headquarters and terminus of the NYMR), and in return, the nursery is supplied with moss from the moors for the hundreds of hanging baskets Graham and his staff prepare each year for the Eastern Region stations. The nursery also has the job of providing the floral arrangements for the numerous special events, such as exhibitions and city festivals that British Rail become involved in up and down the country.

If you are travelling on Eastern Region and the floral decorations catch your eye at a station you can be pretty sure that Graham Warner and Poppleton Nurseries have had a hand in them. They have also contributed to the community involvement at many stations. It is just possible that the South of England rail network may get their own nurseries at some future date, and consultations are in progress towards this end. Harry Hoyle was a well-known gardener at the nursery during its expansion in earlier years. Graham has been at the nursery since 1979 and he has seen many changes and on numerous occasions, although on the verge of closure, has fought battles to prove its worth and usefulness to the railway.

POPPLETON STATION

Being as close as it is to the Poppleton nurseries it is no wonder that the station and its flower-beds should look so colourful.

Separated from Graham Warner's plantation by the level-crossing, the station obviously benefits from his touch. The country-style station building has been recently redecorated, and this shows off the glass canopy in particular to advantage.

There is a large wooden garden seat alongside one of the flower-beds, which adds to the overall cared-for appearance.

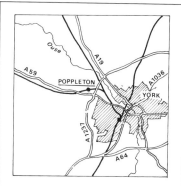

POPPLETON
Opened 1848
East & West Yorkshire
Junction Railway

This line runs from York to Knaresborough and possessed four near-identical stations with remarkably large main buildings, containing accommodation for passengers and living quarters for the station-master that were equally spacious. The other stations on the line were smaller. The plain brick of Poppleton is enlivened by stone-cased doors and windows, with a hooded stone roundel by way of decoration in the main gable. Later on a generous glass-and-iron lean-to awning was added to the platform side, forming a kind of apron, although, in customary fashion, passengers on the opposite platform had to make-do with a small wooden waiting-room.

Graham and the author admiring the nurseries' flowers

SAFETY FIRST PRESERVED

by Peter Howard

Throughout the length and breadth of this country there are many preserved railway lines that have, in most cases, been rebuilt from near-derelict state by a dedicated band of railway enthusiasts through sheer hard work and perseverance and often against almost insurmountable odds.

Apart from the refurbishment of rolling-stock and engines, often from near-rusty hulks, trackbeds, track, drainage ditches, bridges, signals and many other odds and ends of equipment have all had to be rebuilt from basics.

Eventually, after years of determined endeavour to overcome all the obstacles, the great day arrives, and the railway is reopened to the general public as a working preserved line. It is then a little disconcerting to hear some members of the general public refer to the staff as 'overgrown schoolkids playing with a large trainset', especially as the vast majority of them are unpaid volunteers giving up their weekends and quite often annual holidays to work on the railway. Perhaps it is only natural that some people are unaware of the problems in running a preserved railway. I would like to try and put right some preconceived ideas that the general public may have, and explain the very strict Government-controlled rules and regulations under which the railways are run, ensuring that the public travel on those lines in total safety.

The overall responsibility for the condition of, and safe travel on the railways of this country, both British Rail and the preserved lines, rests with the Secretary of State for Transport, but he delegates the rail safety functions to the Railway Inspectorate. This organisation has many inspectors who travel widely to ensure the various operating staff keep their particular railway up to standard, and comply with all the rules and regulations enforced by law.

When a group of people wish to create a preserved railway line from a length of old discarded British Rail trackbed, with the idea of opening it as a working railway carrying the general public, they have to liaise from the start with the Department of Transport. Inspectors are sent from the Railway Inspectorate to talk to the company involved, check their suitability for the task in hand, and thoroughly examine the plans and route of the proposed railway. After several visits and lengthy consultations, and if those plans still stand up, a Public Enquiry will be held at which all the local residents along the route of the proposed line can vent their feelings. If the Secretary of State for Transport then decides that the proposed railway will not cause too much environmental damage, and that the people involved have the ability to raise the necessary finance, and then construct and run the railway, he will award them a Light Railway Order. This is the authority for the company involved to go ahead with the construction of the railway, and its eventual running, and lays down the precise conditions under which that railway must be built and operated. It states precisely where that railway will start and finish, and the exact route that it must take. At all stages of the construction visits are made by the Inspectorate to ensure that all the rules and regulations are complied with, that the standard of the railway's trackbed and track are as prescribed, and that all relevant buildings and stations are sited correctly and up to the necessary building standards. Rolling-stock and locomotives are inspected regularly to ensure that they are rebuilt correctly at each stage and to the exacting standards required. Only after the locomotives have been rebuilt to the satisfaction of the British Rail Inspectors will they be awarded an Operating Certificate, and that only lasts for a certain number of years when the whole process has to be gone through again.

Under the Light Railway Order a preserved railway company is given considerable leeway to decide their own method of operating the railway, and each company draws up its own set of rules peculiar to its own needs, but these have to be agreed and approved by the Railway Inspectorate, plus also the speed limits, and the frequency and number of trains that can be run at any one time.

As work progresses on the railway, notice has to be taken of the Health & Safety Acts and Provisions governing working conditions of the railway personnel, and also the buildings and facilities for the operation of the railway and convenience of the general public. Then the local Health Authority have to be consulted and satisfied regarding catering facilities supplied for the general public and working staff. They also govern the type of sanitary provisions for general use.

As you can see, every aspect of the railway is governed by rules and regulations which have to be complied with, and when the railway eventually starts running services and carrying the general public even more rules and regulations apply – a daunting prospect. These rules and regulations are so numerous and so intricate that most of the preserved railways have banded together to acquire professional advisers to sort out all the legal 'jargon' to keep the companies involved on the right side of the law.

So next time you sit in the railway carriage of a preserved railway and enjoy a journey, probably hauled by a rebuilt steam-engine, please spare a thought for the hours of hard work put in by the dedicated enthusiasts who have made your journey possible. They don't like to be thought of as 'overgrown schoolkids playing with a large trainset', they are professional people carrying out a very responsible job in running a very professional railway, and of course they enjoy themselves too, just as they hope you will enjoy your journeys on the railway for many years to come.

Peter Howard, a retired British Airways Captain, has been a railway enthusiast for over fifty years and is a member of several railway preservation societies.

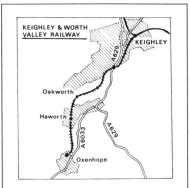

KEIGHLEY & WORTH
VALLEY RAILWAY

KEIGHLEY

Oakworth

Haworth

Oxenhope

KEIGHLEY AND
WORTH VALLEY RAILWAY

My journey to visit the Keighley and Worth Valley Railway began in Leeds in a small two-car Metro train. I don't know why one is always amazed to find that within ten minutes of leaving a busy city, you can find yourself in real country but it is always a delightful surprise. This Leeds to Skipton and the now famous Settle to Carlisle line soon gives you glimpses of thick foliage, rivers, streams and the Leeds and Liverpool canal with its extraordinary five-tier lock.

Shipley Junction between Leeds and Keighley is of a high architectural standard and also has a very handsome signal-box. On arriving at the British Rail platform at Keighley you cross over to the KWVR side of the station by way of a covered ramp. Here you will instantly find all the paraphernalia one normally associates with a preserved railway company – a smart bookstall and brightly coloured hanging baskets, all giving a feeling of well-being. Of course any preserved railway has to be run efficiently and with a high degree of safety measures, just as any other line, but you do generally feel that once you arrive into the atmosphere of a preservation society's station you are stepping back in time.

On Saturday 13th April 1867 Worth Valley was in festive mood. After a few setbacks, including a cow which apparently ate the surveyor's plans, the people of the area had finally got their railway. There were so many people who wanted to travel on the first train from Keighley to Haworth that extra coaches were added and almost immediately the extra load caused the engine to get stuck on the steep gradient out of Keighley Station. Bands played and people feasted on that great day, which provided them with a railway from Keighley to Oxenhope.

Railway mania gripped the country in the 1840s but it wasn't until 1861 that consultations took place between local businessmen and the Midland Railway, who owned the line through Keighley, and permission was given for a line to be built from Keighley Station to Oxenhope.

From its opening in 1867 the single-line branch had a successful career and was still carrying around 130,000 passengers annually when it ceased operations ninety-five years later. The original Worth Valley Railway Company eventually sold out to the Midland Railway which itself became part of the London Midland and Scottish Railway in 1923. Finally in 1948 the country's rail network was nationalised and by the late 1950s British Railways proposed closing the Worth Valley branch on the grounds that it was no longer a viable concern. As with other such lines the cost of operating it was outstripping its usefulness and there were alternative means of transport available. The line eventually closed for passengers in December 1961 and for freight in June 1962.

Even before the last British Rail passenger train had run, activity commenced in an attempt to save the Worth Valley Railway. An open committee meeting was held at which correspondence with British Rail was discussed along with the possibility of obtaining a locomotive and

coaches. Local businessmen seemed to be favourably disposed to the idea of keeping the branch open, but there were two problems which had to be tackled before a full service could be restored to the branch. As with many other societies around the country who were proposing to preserve some of the small branch lines, negotiations with British Rail were long, protracted and frustrating for all concerned. To be fair to British Rail, they had suddenly found themselves in a situation that was slightly foreign to them – they knew how to close a line, but now from various parts of the country societies were wanting to reopen them – and they had to tread very carefully, especially if the line had been left idle for a while. There were stringent safety measures to be observed for one thing and the legal implications of the whole project had to be studied very carefully.

The second problem was capital. The Society asked its solicitor to draw up a scheme whereby it would purchase the branch over a forty-nine-year period at £1,000 per annum or, alternatively, by means of an outright payment of £30,000. Whilst it had always hoped to take over the branch without getting involved with large finance, the Society had made enquiries and been offered a low-interest five-year loan of £18,000 by the Bowater Organisation. In addition, various local people had shown interest in purchasing some of the branch's assets, such as warehouses which the

Keighley Station

35

Society thought it would not need. If necessary the Society felt that it could raise the £30,000.

Eventually British Rail and the Keighley and Worth Valley Railway Society drew up a contract of sale. The British Rail Inspector, Colonel Robertson, OBE, was very helpful to the Society, but admitted that the long negotiations that had taken place had been the most complex he had ever dealt with.

In 1968 the Keighley to Oxenhope branch line was ready to open again, and on 29th June of that year, on a sunny afternoon, the first train left Keighley for Oxenhope, with the Mayor of Keighley, Alderman Waterhouse, on board. There was much to be done now – stations that had been left derelict had to be restored, platforms and tracks high in weeds had to be cleared, but all the protracted negotiations now seemed worthwhile and the volunteers and small band of seasonal paid staff worked long hours in all weathers to restore the line to its former glory. In fact they have done, and are continuing to do more than that: now you can take a steam train for your journey down the line to Oxenhope or you may like to enjoy the comfortable small diesel rail buses and whichever you choose I'm sure you'll have a delightful journey, as I did.

The next station down the line from Keighley is Ingrow West, the 'West' was to distinguish it from Ingrow East which was on the now defunct line out of Keighley to Halifax. Ingrow West was a completely derelict station when the Society took over the line, so when an exact replica was found at Foulridge on the closed Colne to Skipton line it was purchased and moved brick by brick and rebuilt at Ingrow. It is now a superb little station, beautifully restored inside and out, with the large flower-beds surrounding the station, now starting to blossom in profusion. Large brass oil-lamps are ranged all along the platform, and apparently in winter the scene is quite something, particularly on those evenings when the Father Christmas and Carol Service trains travel the line. The large wrought-iron gates to the entrance of the station were donated by Sainsbury's when a supermarket was built on the site of the old Keighley Midland Goods Depot. The station-master here, Stuart Mellin is very proud of his award-winning station, and so he should be. While you are at Ingrow you should try and spend a while in the Vintage Carriages Trust Museum where Victorian and Edwardian carriages are displayed. Further down the line is the smallest station in Britain – Damems. The platform, only long enough to take one coach, is high above the shallow reaches of the River Worth. This pretty little station has a delightful signal-box and the tiniest waiting-room and booking-office. The platform area is surrounded by flowers, rock plants and hanging baskets. Now it's on to *The Railway Children*. Oakworth was used first of all for the television version of the classic story in 1968 and then again for the feature film of the same name, directed by my old friend Lionel Jeffries, and starring another pal of mine, Bernard Cribbins. It really is a delightful station, still in the pre-1914 condition, and lit by gas lamps inside and out. It has won an award for the best-preserved station. One piece of unusual memorabilia on the platform is the coffin trolley; it also has a wonderful assortment of genuine old metal adverts all along the platform. Jim Shipley, the assistant station-master, is a busy man, having to cope with

the level-crossing gates and signalling as well as his platform duties. If you should catch him when he's got the kettle on you'll be invited to join him in a cup of tea.

On to Haworth and Brontë country. The station has had a small extension in keeping with the original and is one of the busiest stations on the line. Here you will find the main souvenir shop on the Keighley and Worth Valley Railway, full of books, videos, models and reproductions of memorabilia, and all presided over by the shop manager, Bernard Bowdler, who is also a keen and excellent amateur photographer. You can also visit the large engine-shed to watch the huge beasts getting up steam for their day's work or being put to bed after it. This shed was originally built by the one-time owners, the Midland Railway, for storing the wool that was a growing trade in the area. The 'Top Field' is situated between Haworth and the terminus Oxenhope, and is so called because of its association with *The Railway Children*. This is where you will also catch a glimpse of the footpath that runs past 'Three Chimneys', the house which was used for the exterior shots in the filming of the story. A delightful stream runs alongside the line and is a favourite picnic spot. You'll get a wave from the children eating their sandwiches on a sunny day.

And into Oxenhope. Much has been done here by the local community in making new flower-beds and a picnic area alongside the return loop. The Local Authority has also helped with a fine carpark layout that also leads down to the carriage maintenance and restoration building, where visitors are always welcome. There is a gift shop on the station, which is geared more to children than railway enthusiasts, manned by jolly-faced Jack Rowell who sports a Santa-style beard. If you feel like a sit-down and snack you can do just that in the buffet car in the siding adjoining the station, and do try their freshly ground coffee, it's delicious. Oxenhope, as all other stations on the line with the exception of Ingrow West (I've mentioned the oil-lamps there) has original gas-lamps for its platform illumination. The interiors of all the stations are excellent, with gleaming brass and polished wood, and real coal fires in the waiting-rooms. The whole line is a credit to the tremendous efforts of the volunteer and paid workers of the Keighley and Worth Valley Railway . . . off we go now, back again to Keighley and wherever the mood takes you after that.

THE RAILWAY CHILDREN

by Bernard Cribbins

Filming *The Railway Children* reminded me of what steam railways were all about. When I was a kid the only time we went on a train was when we went on our annual holidays from Oldham in Lancashire, where I lived, to either Southport, New Brighton or Blackpool. I remember we would be all packed up with our little cardboard suitcases and we'd get the tram down to Mumps Station in Oldham – I think it's probably gone now. From there you got the train to Manchester which is seven miles away, and then you'd get the big train to Blackpool which is all of fifty-odd miles. It took half a day then, now you'd do it by car in little more than an hour.

The thing I remember particularly is that when you got off the train our parents would say 'Why don't you say thank you to the driver.' He would always be hanging out of his cab wiping his hands on a piece of oily cotton waste, and we'd say 'Thank you very much mister'. He'd reply 'That's all right lad, have a good holiday,' and off we'd go. I used to love saying thank you to the driver. This fellow would be smiling away, and all he'd done was drive a train for fifty miles, but he was the guv'nor.

When we did *The Railway Children* on the Worth Valley line the first things that came back were the noise and the smell, particularly the smell, because I remember also as a kid standing on iron bridges over railway tracks and allowing the steam train to go underneath and just envelop you in that sort of sulphur – very good for the chest I'm sure! Another smell I remember was the one you got from the big thick leather window straps, quite a strong smell. We used to let the windows down with a bang and then watch the other passengers jump with surprise at the noise.

We had two or three engines in the film, the main one was a little green pannier engine. When you got close to it it was very, very hot indeed, not surprising when you think of all that steam and burning coal inside.

Driving a big engine must have been the most awful existence I think. Can you imagine going eight hours from London to Edinburgh with *The Flying Scotsman*! Everything's hard in a steam cab, nothing soft in there at all. It's not like sitting in a car, everything is hot, hard metal and your backside would be freezing if it's winter and the front side of you would be absolutely roasting hot. When you're hungry you open up the fire box, wipe the shovel, put your bacon and eggs on it, put it in and – wonderful – the best bacon and eggs in the world, so they tell me. They were always heroes those cab crews. 'What does your dad do?' 'He's an engine driver.' 'Wow!' I never wanted to be an engine driver but it's one of the things kids always wanted to do – to be in charge of a great monster.

I remember talking about it with the guard on the film of *The Railway Children*, Mr Mitchell, and we were saying that it is the nearest thing man has produced to the human body inasmuch as you have got all that

39

piping which is carrying water (like veins), you've got the great engine, the fire box that you have got to feed with fuel, and that is then turned into energy and rushes around and drives the rods. It is like a great big human being, a hot human being. But it was an amazing invention the big, big steam-engine, fifty to sixty feet long, and all that coal. Fantastic – really wonderful! The modern diesel engine, which is just a big engine housed in a box, hasn't got the same romance about it. Steam wasn't as efficient perhaps, but they used to get you there didn't they!

The steam train is just a romantic memory really I suppose. I'm so glad the societies are keeping them going just to show modern day children what was commonplace.

I met Mr Mitchell again (he is now Chairman of the Preservation Society in Keighley), and we were discussing the origins of the steam years. They came along with the Industrial Revolution, and were there for a particular purpose, to take raw material in and bring out the goods, employed hundreds of thousands of people, and changed the lives of so many who lived along their routes. They held communities together too. When Dr Beeching chopped bits off, he destroyed an awful lot of rural communication. That little train used to go through once a day, and you could put your chickens on, and they would be taken out four stations down. I remember also as a kid you would see all the pigeon fanciers (they probably still do it on ordinary trains, I don't know). There would be enormous baskets of racing pigeons that would be put on in Oldham and they would be shot off to New Brighton or wherever and then released at a certain time, and back to the loft.

It seemed to be a much more personal service somehow on the steam railway. Now there are more people, and it needs to be automated somewhat, but it has been depersonalised hasn't it! Many problems on the railways nowadays have been self-induced. Unmanned stations being a major one.

Another thing I miss are net luggage racks, comfortable to sleep on if you couldn't find a seat, like hammocks – you can't sleep in today's metal ones. And all those lovely posters and bevelled mirrors. I suppose they were always being vandalised. Thank goodness the preserved railways were able to get hold of some while there were still a few about. The station-master used to do everything on the station if he had to, like Perks, the character I played in *The Railway Children*. They wrote it in that he would do everything, take tickets, close doors, dash down and open level-crossing gates etc. And there was always a station house he lived in, which was either adjacent or very near. The Keighley and Worth Valley Railway was a mill line built by the wool people up there. The mill was water-driven as there was a stream running past it. The whole of the line was surrounded by beautiful and atmospheric scenery, it still is. Perks's station, Oakworth, was a lovely station. It had a delightful little room which was the station-master's office, with a cast-iron grate.

I stayed with my wife Gillian at the Devonshire Arms in Bolton Abbey while we were filming, and I used to finish shooting, come back to the hotel, have a shower and a drink, and then go out and fish for half an hour before dinner. After a day's work in front of the cameras, all rather pleasant and relaxing. I really wouldn't mind doing it all again.

CENTRAL

Geoffrey Hunt, the signalman at Attleborough.

ATTLEBOROUGH

The station which is between Thetford and Wymondham on the Ely to Norwich line is in the process of putting the colour back into the flower-beds around the station. The signalman is responsible for what has been done already and has certainly made a fine start.

The station buildings are leased out, and the forecourt is really the responsibility of the lessees. In the middle of the forecourt, which was part of the original goods yard, there is a huge mound of ash and coal waste from the steam period on the line, and it is hoped that this will provide a base for a huge central rose garden. Let us hope this will be developed soon – it would be such a wonderful focal point for the station, and would add considerably to our friend the signalman's good work.

THE EAST SUFFOLK RAILWAY

The East Suffolk Railway line, and it is still known as that in the area, is part of the British Rail network. Before nationalisation it was part of the London and North Eastern, and before that the Great Eastern which took over the East Suffolk Railway line.

The Ipswich to Lowestoft branch was once, like many of the other busy lines in Suffolk and Norfolk, a community railway linking small market towns and fishing villages. The stations used to have their resident station-masters who were kings in their castles and very much a part of what the railways stood for.

Like many other lines in the counties, it was threatened with closure in the mid 1960s, but a campaign organised by a Woodbridge lady saved this one. However, large economies had to be made and station-masters had to go. There stations were closed and tickets were purchased from a ticket collector on the trains. The whole signal system of the single-track line was then concentrated in one box at Saxmundham.

After some time British Rail offered to lease the station buildings to commercial businesses. Woodbridge, for instance, is now a guest-house and taxi-hire firm. By the way if you have time to saunter round Woodbridge, it really is a beautiful little town. Saxmundham Station was also leased out, as is the little station of Melton which houses a taxi firm, a coal merchants and coal-fire appliance showroom.

The East Suffolk Railway line passes through varied scenery, including the Broads, and Wild Life Trusts to the seaside at Lowestoft. On my last visit to the line I did notice a certain lack of care being given to some of the leasehold stations except for Melton. This station is now over 120 years old, and it is looked after by the local branch of the Women's Institute of which Mrs Opie is the driving force. They do a good job·here, and ensure that the platform is kept clean and all the flower tubs, situated along the platform, are well cared for and planted with a great variety of blooms. With the help of local nurseryman Mr Swann they have also cleared and planted up an overgrown garden where the trees and shrubs are now well-established. If you get a chance you'll enjoy the riverside scene opposite the platform side of the station where you'll be greeted with a host of ducks and geese in search of food.

During the Second World War Melton Station played host to King George VI when he used it as a stop on his way to visit nearby aerodromes. I'll bet most of the country branch lines have their own particular anecdotes to relate.

THETFORD

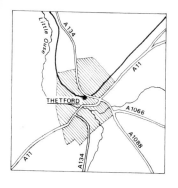

The semaphore signals at Thetford

The old settlement of Thetford was built astride the Icknield Way, the ancient trade route, and beside the River Thet and Little Ouse. In the ninth century the Danes made Thetford their capital, and later it became the See of the Bishops of East Anglia and the residence of its early kings. Thomas Paine was born here in the eighteenth century and will always be remembered for his 'Bill of Rights' and the part he played in the founding of the American nation.

In the twentieth century, 1968 to be exact, along came *Dad's Army*, led by one Captain George Mainwaring. For nine years his Home Guard platoon was based at the Bell Hotel in Thetford from which he carried out devious sorties on the nearby Stanford Battle area and neighbouring villages. His escapades were often interrupted by a rather off-hand Air Raid Warden, an argumentative Vicar and a fussy Verger. This motley crew with their accompanying technicians and aides such as make-up and wardrobe personnel would arrive at Thetford Station from London having changed at Ely on to the Norwich train. The sight of Thetford's signal-box and semaphore signals (very few left on British Rail now) were familiar to *Dad's Army* as they crossed the footbridge from the down platform for their battles in Thetford, planned in advance by David Croft and Jimmy Perry.

WYMONDHAM

WYMONDHAM, THETFORD and ATTLEBOROUGH
Opened 1845
Norfolk Railway
Listed Grade II

Although it was built by the Norwich & Brandon Railway, the line became part of the somewhat larger Norfolk Railway shortly before opening. The original stations possess remarkable variety in style, of which Wymondham, architecturally, is the least distinguished, being curiously muted considering the character of the ancient market town it served and the magnificent abbey. Its walls of Norfolk flint, with prominent brick rustication around the doors and windows and a steeply gabled centrepiece on the front, do, however, harmonise well with the local tradition. The decorated flat platform awnings were added later by the Great Eastern Railway, of which the Norfolk Railway eventually became part. The massive brick goods shed, which was a later addition (there was a similar one at Brandon) more than makes up for the modesty of the passenger station.

The original building at Thetford, however, was entirely different. Again in flint, it was built in an elaborate Jacobean style and was considered sufficiently noteworthy for the *Illustrated London News* to include an engraving with its account of the

This station gave me more inspiration than perhaps any others that I have seen on my travels. I happened to be in Norfolk in 1988 and was told that a gentleman by the name of David Turner had taken a lease on Wymondham Station from British Rail. His idea was to refurbish it and use it as the headquarters of his piano business.

David was well-known for his interest in the environment and the restoration of property in his home village of nearby Ashwellthorpe. When I first saw the station it looked like a depot for bricks, cement, plaster etc., with wood beams and steel RSJs cluttering up both exterior and interior. His far-sightedness, life-long ambition and enthusiasm in wanting to restore the station to its former glory was quite catching and the people of this little market town were quick to support him, as was British Rail. Just one year later, in October 1989, the transformation was almost complete, and David invited me to perform the reopening ceremony. For twenty years or mre the buildings had lain idle and had deteriorated in every aspect. The platforms were still used for people travelling on the line but tickets were bought on the train, as is the custom on most Norfolk and Suffolk lines.

The reopening of this once-busy junction (you changed there for East Dereham, Wells-next-the-Sea and Kings Lynn) was a quite wonderful day for David Turner. Things didn't go quite according to plan, but few occasions such as this normally do, but what an occasion it was. The local brass band greeted nearly a thousand people assembled in the large car-park where David welcomed everybody. He then handed over to the local vicar for a brief history of the station. This caused the first hiccup of the day. The wind was so strong that the sound system worked only spasmodically, rather like the comedian Norman Collier with his impersonation of the Chairman of a Working Men's Club with a faulty microphone. This, as you can imagine, caused a certain amount of merriment with the crowd, but it was nothing compared to the mirth created by my pulling the cord attached to the covering over the stone plaque high on the wall, announcing that 'The station was reopened by actor Bill Pertwee'! The cord broke in my hand leaving the stone still covered. An extending ladder was called for and I climbed up and uncovered the notice by hand, to the cheers of the crowd and yet another chorus of 'Who do you think you're kidding Mr Hitler' from the mass band.

It was quite obvious that there was going to be a tight squeeze in the guest marquee David had had erected for refreshments. The people who had partaken of their glass of wine and plate of grub were rather trapped by the people coming in, and vice versa, and what with the wind blowing the marquee about, there was still further confusion.

However, the popularity of David's station has gone from strength to strength. The old waiting-room is a magnificent piano showroom, complete with crystal chandeliers, and the caretaker's apartment, previously the station-master's quarters, has been beautifully furnished, and David's sitting-room and office is like something out of a Noël Coward play. The

opening of the line. The building still stands, next to the present entrance building which was added in 1889 in a style typical of the Great Eastern in that period, when the platform awnings were also added.

Attleborough, on the other hand, although much plainer, has distinctively Tudor characteristics, its prominent stone door and window hoods contrasting with the brickwork, while the adjoining two-storey house has three bold gables overlooking the platform.

old Buffet is now a handsome room decorated in the style of a Pullman Dining Car. The Buffet is called 'The Brief Encounter', and it is decorated with pictures from the film of that name starring Trevor Howard and Celia Johnson. Railway memorabilia is to be found in great abundance in the corridor leading into the piano showroom and it is certainly worth looking at.

During a recent filming session in Norfolk I took the cast of *You Rang, M'Lord?* over to the station, and we had a wonderful evening in David's company, starting off with drinks at the tables on the platform. We then had a jolly meal in the Buffet, complete with wine, all handled by Peter Barker and his staff. Incidentally, while we were there Su Pollard, one of the stars of *You Rang, M'Lord?* bought a piano for her London home as a reminder of her visit. The station is now on the list of Tourist Board attractions and many people actually break their journey to and from Norwich and Ely just to have a look around or partake of coffee, lunch, tea or dinner in this most unusual atmosphere.

David I know is most appreciative of all the help he has had from British Rail, mainly in decorating the station canopies and very fine and unusual footbridge. I think British Rail in the Anglia region is very forward-looking with good ideas. The up platform is leased to the Plasmas Brick Co and David helps to look after their floral decorations.

The branch line to East Dereham is still in existence, but the station buildings themselves have been sold off. David Turner is now involved in helping to preserve this branch for the future. The line could be used for light railway purposes to see some of the beautiful countryside in this area. Knowing David as I do I am sure if it is at all possible we will once again see the odd train or two travelling up to East Dereham and back again.

If you are in the vicinity of this delightful town of Wymondham do pop in to the station. I'm sure you'll enjoy your visit.

'Music Maestro, please!' The piano salesroom at Wymondham Station

46

Above: A convivial evening with David Turner and the cast and crew of *You Rang M'Lord?* at The Brief Encounter Restaurant

Left: The re-opening of the restored station by the author.

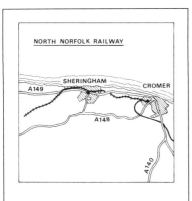

NORTH NORFOLK RAILWAY

Sheringham Station

THE NORTH NORFOLK RAILWAY 'THE POPPY LINE'

My introduction to the North Norfolk Railway was in the early 1970s when BBC television's *Dad's Army* film unit arrived at Sheringham Station to make an episode called 'The Royal Train'. The actors and technical crew stayed at a large hotel on the sea-front at Cromer, and were transported daily to Sheringham and Weybourne stations for 'work'. Although all filming is tiring, working mainly very long hours, this sequence of events on the North Norfolk Railway was as pleasant a time as any during the nine-year run of the television series.

The preserved line between Sheringham and Holt is part of a huge network of Norfolk rail links that were literally wiped out during the 1960s' closures. One of the original companies in the area, the Midland and Great Northern, was nicknamed the Muddle and Get Nowhere, so perhaps some of the rail links in Norfolk should have been tidied up, but not slashed to pieces.

One of the original lines that has survived in part, due to preservation, was the Melton Constable to Sheringham and Cromer line, then owned by the Eastern and Midland Railway (the 'Muddle and Get Nowhere' took over later). All the railways in Norfolk and neighbouring Suffolk linked up with London and other major cities, even though you had to change trains a few times, so it must have been devastating when suddenly the lines of communication, used for personal and business purposes to and from the market towns and resorts of East Anglia, were reduced to practically nothing. To look at a map of then and now is quite a revelation.

From the large junction of Melton Constable, south of Sheringham, you could travel to practically anywhere in the United Kingdom. The Midland and Great Northern company did a great deal for the people of Melton Constable. They built houses, schools and facilities such as gas works, water storage towers, recreation grounds and bowling greens. As far as the town of Melton was concerned the M&GN certainly didn't deserve the nickname that they'd been given.

In the early 1900s the area was one of the busiest in Britain with holidaymakers, particularly from the Midlands, crammed into express trains on their way to the popular seaside resorts of Cromer and Yarmouth. In 1923 the company came under the joint management of the London Midland and Scottish and the London and North Eastern Railways, although the day-to-day running of the lines in Norfolk were still under the influence of the Midland and Great Northern, and from 1936 until the nationalisation of the railway system in 1948 the London and North Eastern became the sole owners.

The line from Melton Constable to Sheringham was closed in 1964 but the rest of the line from Sheringham to Cromer remained open, although British Rail have built a small halt at Sheringham across the road from the original station, which is where the North Norfolk Railway comes in – or to put it another way, came in – to the lives of many local residents and railway enthusiasts. The newly formed company wanted to purchase the section of the line from Sheringham to Weybourne, establishing headquarters at the former, but with all the legal issues and the hundred and one other problems to sort out with the project, the company was just not able to act in time to stop the tracks and sidings being taken up at Weybourne and also part way to Sheringham.

But once the company took possession, volunteers started relaying the track for the line and the sidings. It was not until the mid 1970s that the Light Railway Order was granted to carry passengers, a year or two after we had used Sheringham and Weybourne for the making of the *Dad's Army* television programme I have mentioned.

Sheringham Station is a very good example of Victorian and Edwardian architecture, and the building has a W H Smith bookstall, souvenir shop and buffet, all now familiar sights on preserved railways.

Weybourne is a typical country station with a decorative canopy and station-master's office, booking-hall and buffet. There are several sidings with locomotive sheds and workshops adjacent to the station and a signal-box which controls the traffic in and out of Weybourne. The journey between Sheringham and Weybourne passes through some lovely scenery, and it's good to know that most of this land can never be developed.

Soon after leaving Sheringham you can see on the sea side of the line the eighteen-hole golf course, and on the inland side the village of Upper Sheringham. You also have a view of the magnificent Sheringham Hall Estate with its beautiful gardens, which are particularly spectacular in the spring. After a considerable climb you then glimpse the North Sea and on a breezy day those great 'white horses'. After levelling out it's then downhill for a while, and I remember well this stretch of line – I nearly had an accident on the pump trolley we were using for the filming of 'The Royal Train'!

It is then followed by another climb past Deadman's Hill on the seaward side, so named because the Norfolk victims of the great plague were buried there. Not far from here the experienced bridge engineer David Pinkerton tragically died after an accidental fall shortly before the reconstruction of a bridge over the A149 road was completed in 1984.

The line carries on almost all the way uphill to Weybourne, from where there is an interesting short journey to Holt, the North Norfolk Railway's new station, which is presently the end of the line. Holt is surrounded by Forestry Commission land and gravel pits which were used in the making of the original railway. Gresham Public School is here, and a short walk or bus journey will take you into the town itself, with its elegant Georgian buildings.

If the passengers who travel on the North Norfolk Railway have as much fun as we did when we were filming there they'll really enjoy their visit to the railway, as I know many people already have during its sixteen years' existence as a passenger-carrying railway.

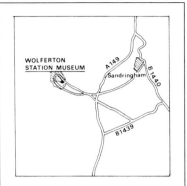

WOLFERTON STATION MUSEUM

One of the most famous stations in Britain is now a museum and tourist attraction of rather special significance. The museum focuses particularly on five generations of the monarchy who travelled to and from the station for a hundred years.

As you enter the wide forecourt entrance with its gravelled drive, wrought-iron gates and period lamps, you are entering not just a part of railway history but also one of past grandeur. This forecourt was the scene of military parades complete with bands when visiting Heads of State were once welcomed to Sandringham by our Royal families. The station is just two and a quarter miles from Sandringham House in Norfolk, the house and estate that was originally bought by Queen Victoria for her son the Prince of Wales, later Edward VII in 1862. The plans to build the Kings Lynn to Hunstanton line of which Wolferton was a part were passed in 1861, which is why the station and its surrounds are a piece of freehold land amidst what was to become the large estate of Sandringham. The land the Wolferton Museum stands on still enjoys its freehold to this day.

The whole line including Wolferton Station was closed in the mid 1960s along with many others in Norfolk and Suffolk. When it was sold by British Rail it was bought as a private residence by Eric and Herta Walker. Eric had been a railway employee, and during that time had collected a great amount of railway memorabilia, including many items connected with the monarchy. He therefore decided to turn the station into a museum to display his collection. After his death his son Roger moved into the premises to carry on the family 'business'. Roger bought a small residence nearby for his young family, but continued to run the museum for the enjoyment of visitors. With inheritance tax to pay he and his wife have found it difficult to always show a profit, but are determined to make sure that Wolferton Station Museum will survive. It is only recently that signs have been allowed to be erected on the main Kings Lynn to Hunstanton Road, the A149, indicating where the museum is situated. It really is in the most delightful setting, and even the drive off the main road to it is quite charming.

The history that surrounds this beautiful little station museum is worth preserving for as long as is possible, not just for this generation but also for the future. The people who have passed through it are part of our living history, not just of this country but of many other lands too. You enter the station building from the platform through large double doors which lead into a wide entrance hall and directly opposite at the other end two similar doors open out into the courtyard. On either side of the hall are two retiring rooms designed for Prince Edward, later King, and Princess Alexandra, later his Queen, after whom they have now been named. Both rooms have their own private toilet facilities with much gold leaf edged round the pans (difficult to keep clean because the paint would rub off if it was treated with a caustic material). These buildings on the down platform were built after the original station was erected on the up side of the line. In the museum rooms there are letters and photographs

in abundance, that record visits to the station.

The memorabilia is very much angled to the Edwardian period of the station's history, but there is much to see that reflects the progress of general rail travel too. Among other items on show is the young Victoria's travelling bed, made for her in 1828. In her diary of August 1832 she wrote, 'I was asleep in a minute in my *litile* (her spelling) bed which travels always with me.' A lot of the furniture in Edward's rest-room came out of the royal trains of that period. When Edward and Alexandra travelled to Sandringham they would arrive at Wolferton with their guests (there were many at times), and a short break of a couple of hours would be spent in these rooms while the staff unloaded the luggage on to handcarts which they pushed up to Sandringham House. When the station got the all-clear that the porters and attendants had arrived and unpacked the luggage the royal party would move off from the station, after inspecting the Guard of Honour, accompanied with rousing choruses from the military bands. When Queen Alexandra was meeting a royal guest off the

The Royal flush – Queen Alexandra's private toilet.

Above right, the red carpet treatment at Wolferton

train she would make sure tea was ready for them, which would be served in the small garden adjoining the station.

Some of the dignitaries who came to Wolferton during its hundred-year association with Sandringham were the King and Queen of Spain, Kaiser Wilhelm II – HRH Prince Henry of Battenberg – Kings of The Helenes and Belgium and Portugal – Crown Princes of Norway and Sweden, Roumania and Siam, H H Prince Albert of Schleswig-Holstein, etc., etc. Actors and actresses including Sir Seymour Hicks, Ellalaine Terris, and comedians such as Dan Leno who were commanded to entertain at Sandringham. Even Rasputin arrived at Wolferton demanding 'to see the King' (he was sent packing by the station-master), and the notorious Mrs Simpson was also a visitor. The short fifteen-and-a-quarter-mile branch line from Kings Lynn to Hunstanton must have seen more royal trains arriving and departing than any other line in the country. Wolferton received the body of George V for the journey to London when he died at Sandringham in January 1936. His son George VI was also borne to London from the station when he too died in the Norfolk retreat in February 1952.

When it finally closed, the building was left derelict for some time, and British Rail tried to get permission to knock the buildings down and put a development of bungalows on the site. Thank goodness common sense prevailed, and the work of restoration by Eric Walker began. More facts and details can be found in the station museum guide which you can buy along with souvenirs in the little shop. Mr and Mrs Walker will be delighted to show you around, or organise tours for schoolchildren and other societies. Do pay them a visit, it's so worthwhile.

GREAT BENTLEY

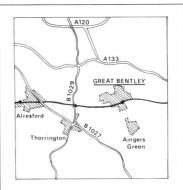

'Are we going to see the gnome station Mummy?' That is what local children say when they are taking a trip on the Colchester line in Essex which runs to and from Clacton, or Walton-on-the-Naze. Great Bentley is well-known for its gnomes. They are everywhere on the station platform gardens and I don't know whose idea it was, or who looks after 'the dear little souls', but whoever it is should be congratulated on not only bringing this very unusual scene to the railway traveller but also for looking after the flowers on the station and keeping it clean and tidy.

The main building on the down side of Great Bentley is practically the same structure that was built by the Tendring Hundred Railway Company, the first owners of the line, when the station was opened in 1866 and it is similar to several others on the same route. It was originally called Bentley Green, but the name was changed in 1878. The Tendring Company was formed in 1859 to build a short railway from Colchester's port at Hythe to Wivenhoe where larger ships could berth. It was extended by degrees between 1863 and 1867 to Walton-on-the-Naze. In 1882 a second branch was opened from Thorpe-le-Soken, which was between Bentley and Walton, to Clacton-on-Sea. This resort was just beginning to gain in popularity, and although quite near Frinton and Walton it was catering more for the day-tripper with its amusement arcades, funfairs and pier. I did some of my early theatre work at Clacton, including concerts at Billy Butlin's Holiday Camp which catered for thousands of holidaymakers each week, not just during the summer but also at Easter and Christmas.

The original branch line to Clacton was built by the Clacton-on-Sea Railway Company, but in 1883 they and the Tendring Company were bought outright by the Great Eastern Railway which actually operated the line for a percentage of receipts. The station at Frinton on the Walton branch was opened in 1888. The Great Eastern continued to improve the services from London to Walton and Clacton in the early part of this century. The line was certainly a greater benefit to Clacton than Frinton, however, because of the huge amount of day-trippers and bed and breakfast boarders who visited Clacton. Walton and Frinton had always been popular for retired and elderly people.

The branch to Clacton was used as an experimental line when electrification came in 1959 and it was continued into London's Liverpool Street in 1962. Great Bentley's goods yard was closed in the late 1960s when freight traffic was moved more and more by road transport, but passenger traffic has increased and Great Bentley also has the added attraction of its own 'Ideal Gnome Exhibition'!

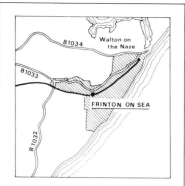

FRINTON-ON-SEA
or 'PERTWEELAND'

I feel ashamed – and if I'd been someone else I would have taken me to task! I have never been to Frinton-on-Sea. 'So what?' you may say. Let me explain. When the Pertwees left France during the Huguenot uprising, a small number of them came to this country, settled in Essex and very soon established themselves in the business of farming. Eventually some families married into the fruit and flower-growing business and the amalgamations carried on fairly steadily. Some of them established allied trades such as corn-chandlery, engineering and marine exploration, and much later on some achieved high-ranking positions in the armed services, in intelligence and the NATO alliance. One or two Pertwees decided to become actors and writers, but we won't talk about them, that's another story anyway.

It appears that when all the hard-working contingent retire most of them go to live in Frinton-on-Sea. At the last count a few years ago the number was seventy. I have certainly been told about Frinton in great detail, and it sounds a delightful spot: there are restrictions on certain types of building developments; you can park in the main street with its large selection of shops and leave your car while you have a cup of coffee or tea without a warning from traffic wardens; there are specialist clock and porcelain shops; picture galleries and a Summer Repertory Theatre, run by my old pal Jack Watling and his family who have made a name for themselves in the commercial theatre and on television all over the world.

The latest asset to the town's well-being is the Frinton and Walton Heritage Trust. They have taken on certain projects which have enhanced some areas that needed looking after, and one of these has been Frinton Station. The station is on one of the branch lines to Walton-on-the-Naze, but it was originally just a halt until a proper station was built in 1888. The new station contained a booking-office, waiting-rooms and storerooms, with a large goods yard and sheds and was built by the Marine Land Company who were developing in the area.

Frinton was slow to develop but then the population was only thirty in 1874 so they obviously didn't want to rush at it. Gradually the town began to rely on the railway for a lot of its needs, including coal, building materials and of course, food. One or two hotels were built as Frinton and the surrounding area became more and more popular with holiday visitors, and a fillip to this in 1904 was the visit of the Duke of Connaught and his family who stayed at the resort.

This line through to Walton-on-the-Naze played a vital part in the Second World War when it was used to carry servicemen and supplies to the large gun emplacements established in the area, which was considered a high-risk part of the coast in the event of a German invasion.

The passenger rail traffic is very much more commuter-orientated nowadays so you would be surprised to learn, as I did, that the Frinton Station and its surrounds had been allowed to get rather shabby. The

The unusual mural at Frinton

passing loopline had been taken up, so making the down platform redundant and the goods yard was closed in 1964. After 1962 trains were electrically powered and everything was nice and cosy until 1982 when passengers had to use a shuttle service to Thorpe-le-Soken, the junction between Frinton and Colchester. This was certainly better news than the suggestion that the line should close altogether. There was also one through-train to London in the morning at 8 a.m. and arriving back at 7 p.m. so things certainly weren't as bad as they could have been. It has now become much easier for residents to commute to London, although I am told that the service still has its hiccups, but I suspect this may be due to the rebuilding of Liverpool Street Station.

The environment of the station was, however, a problem, so in 1985 the Frinton and Walton Heritage Trust decided to take over and with the co-operation of British Rail they have done much to improve its appearance. The entrance to the station has been planted with shrubs and flowers, the waiting-room is carpeted, with comfortable easy chairs, plants and magazines for waiting travellers and a huge mural was painted on the back wall of the disused down-platform waiting-shelter depicting Frinton in Edwardian times.

The Trust's finest hour probably came with the acquisition of the nearby old level-crossing keeper's cottage which they have refurbished. The garden has been beautifully restored and after a lot of time and money being spent on it the cottage is now a small museum and social centre, and coffee mornings are held there once a week when visitors are invited to join them and learn a little more about Frinton-on-Sea. I promise I'm going up there as soon as I can, not just to see Frinton but to have a cup of coffee. As a Huguenot descendant I'm sure they'll make me welcome.

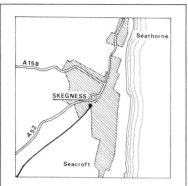

SKEGNESS

John Hassall was a leading commercial artist of his day, but I am sure he never thought that a design for a poster depicting a fisherman bounding along a seaside beach would bring him the fame that it did. He sold the design to the Great Northern Railway Company in 1908 for £12 and the railway reproduced it to advertise Sunday excursions from King's Cross in London to Skegness on the east coast for a return fare of three shillings (15p). This poster with the slogan 'Skegness is SO bracing', thought up by an unknown railway employee, not only sold the excursions but also accelerated the growing popularity of the resort. The 'fisherman' was incorporated in the mayoral chain of office, and in 1934 Hassall was presented with a silver statuette modelled from his painting of the fisherman. This in fact was his first ever visit to Skegness. He did say then that he painted the picture in the hope of selling it as a poster design. In 1939 his name appeared in King George VI's Civil Pensions List which granted him for life the sum of £110 per year in recognition of his services to poster art. The poster went on being used until the Second World War.

The East Lincolnshire Railway run by the Great Northern Railway Company between Boston and Grimsby opened in 1848, but it was another twenty-three years before a branch line between Little Steeping and Firsby was laid to Wainfleet, and then five miles further on to Skegness in 1873. When Skegness Station was opened in July 1873 the population of that village was just three hundred and forty-nine. The branch to Wainfleet had been opened to serve the agricultural interests in the area, but the extension to Skegness was intended to encourage summer trippers from the East Midlands to visit the seaside. Improving wages and better working hours gave factory workers the chance to spend a day by the sea and some even a full week's holiday.

Soon after the opening of the station two thousand trippers arrived in the town in one day. The 'village' was not at that time prepared for such large numbers, and the shops and cafés soon ran out of food. However, men and women rushed to the beaches to take in the bracing air and literally fling themselves into the sea. Bathing machines were dispensed with, and one local resident was prompted to complain that 'men and women in a nude state were disporting themselves in the water in close proximity'.

Lord Scarborough, who owned much of the land in and around Skegness, was feeling the result of the agricultural depression, and so began to sell his land for the development of a large new township that holiday-makers would hopefully come to in their thousands, if not millions. The railway's faith in the future of the resort was confirmed when in one day, during the August Bank Holiday of 1882, it carried more than twenty thousand trippers into the resort, a record for a single day. Shops and refreshment rooms were again cleared of food, and beer was sold from tin baths replenished from buckets. Thousands of struggling people fought their way into the station which the railway had enlarged to cope

with the anticipated extra traffic. It was in this atmosphere of the growing resort that the Great Northern Railway bought Hassall's painting and turned it into the most recognisable poster in Britain. 'Skegness is SO bracing' cemented the realisation that it was 'the place to go'.

A referendum in the town in 1927 resulted in permission being given for the opening of eating places on a Sunday. In the following summer a fairground proprietor, Billy Butlin, was also given permission to open his amusement park on Sunday afternoons. Billy had noticed, particularly on rainy days, that parents were walking round the town with nothing to do once they had left their bed and breakfast accommodation. He thought that the best way to solve the problem of bored and fed-up children and their worried parents (and make him money) would be to put the amusements, accommodation and eating facilities under one roof, and so in 1936 the first Butlin's Holiday Camp was opened at Skegness.

During his reign as the King of the Camps Billy entertained millions of holidaymakers at his other camps which he eventually built in Sussex, Somerset, Essex, Wales and Scotland. The Butlin Red Coat theatre revues were the jumping-off ground for entertainers such as Des O'Connor, Dave Allen, Roy Hudd, Charlie Drake, Terry Scott and many more. Billy gave millions of pounds to charity and was knighted for his efforts in 1964.

Those lads and lassies didn't know what they were starting, when they dashed naked into the sea all those years before.

STRATFORD-UPON-AVON

If Stratford-upon-Avon had had a railway station in William Shakespeare's day he would certainly have used it because 'Will' was an actor as well as a playwright, and actors nearly always travel by train. It goes back to the time when a lot of touring theatrical companies had their own carriages to transport them around the country.

When I arrived at Stratford-upon-Avon Station it was a sunny day, the staff were cheerful and the flower-beds were blooming. The plants are looked after in rotation by the early- and late-turn station staff. Enthusiastic as they are, the staff can only do so much, and the overall upkeep of the buildings is a responsibility that should be borne not only by British Rail but also by the local authorities.

Stratford-upon-Avon is one of the biggest tourist attractions in Britain, and the local administration and businesses should become involved, as happens elsewhere, because they all share in the financial rewards that are brought into the area by visitors, and the station should be part of what's on show in Stratford-upon-Avon. Most people who have visited the town will be aware of Shakespeare's birth place in Henley Street and the Grammar School he attended, both reminders of the Bard, and certainly on the tourists' itinerary, but it is generally known all over the world that the Royal Shakespeare Memorial Theatre on the banks of the River Avon is where the living poet is to be found, with productions every summer of his famous plays.

Our American cousins will always try to take in Harvard House which proudly flies the star-spangled banner. This sixteenth-century timbered building was once owned by the grandparents of John Harvard who founded the University in America.

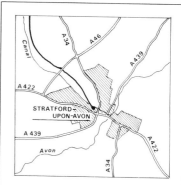

STRATFORD-UPON-AVON
Opened 1863
Great Western Railway

Initially, Stratford had two short-lived terminal stations about half a mile apart. One was at the end of a branch from the Oxford Worcester & Wolverhampton Railway at Honeybourne, opened in 1859, and the other from the Great Western at Hatton, opened in the following year. In 1861 the two lines were connected, and the two stations were replaced by the present one in 1863, by which time the Great Western had absorbed the other company. When the Honeybourne line was closed in 1976, Stratford again became the terminus of a branch. The station's main building is built in a style developed by I. K. Brunel which continued to be used for some years by his successors on the GWR: Italianate, with an overhanging roof forming an awning on both sides. Flanking buildings and broader awnings that were added later now tend to mask the original portion, although to the careful observer it can still be seen.

'Shall I compare thee to a summer's day?'

Steam-train enthusiast Arthur Bostram, who plays the gendarme in the highly successful television series 'Allo 'Allo!, remembers the day he, with many other people, waited at Rugby Central Station for the 'last train' to run on the London Marylebone to Manchester route before it closed. A gleaming green (Southern Railway) locomotive came into view pulling the train and was greeted with loud cheers and applause. After it left the station another engine came into view, a dirty old tank engine, grubby in the extreme, pulling a few goods wagons. On the front of the tank engine, scribbled in chalk, were the words 'positively the last train into Rugby Central'.

This got an even bigger cheer!

GREAT CENTRAL RAILWAY

'A return trip to yesterday' is how the Great Central Preserved Railway describes its activities, and it certainly fulfils that promise. The ever-increasing ambitions of the company to extend their line in the Midlands is certainly within their reach if the staff that I met at Loughborough Central Station have anything to do with it. The existing preserved stretch of line from Loughborough to Rothley is a small part of the once very busy Manchester to London (Marylebone) route owned by the original Great Central Railway.

The Great Central Railway had its origins in the Manchester, Sheffield and Lincolnshire Railway Company. An early General Manager of the Company, Edward Watkin, had great ambitions for linking his railway to various other companies going south and through London to the channel ports and then on to the continent of Europe via a channel tunnel which he proposed to build. This was in the late 1850s, one hundred and thirty years before the present tunnel project which is now coming to fruition, though not to everyone's satisfaction I am sure. However, most of Watkin's schemes were not implemented because most people thought that his ideas would profit him most.

A London extension to the already thriving company was given consideration, but this did not happen until 1899. At that time the name of the company was changed from the MS&LR to the Great Central. Its boast for the new line was 'speed and comfort'. London was now within easy reach for businessmen from Manchester and the stations in between. The railway's engines and rolling-stock were smart and well cared for, and so at least some of Watkin's ambitions had been realised.

In 1923 the Great Central Railway became part of the London and North Eastern Railway, and later still in 1948 British Rail, Eastern Region. By 1950 road transport was playing a bigger part in our lives, both commercially and domestically, and the line became an obvious target for reduction in services, and ten years later eventual closure as other routes into London became more popular and received more attention from British Rail. The last remaining section, Nottingham to Rugby, was closed in 1969.

If you are in Nottingham you will see one remaining piece of the Victoria Station complex on view. It is the station forecourt clock tower now standing outside the huge Victorian Shopping Arcade that was built on the site of the old station. At the time of the final closure a small group of enthusiasts thought it might be possible to preserve the section of the line between Nottingham and Leicester, but the ambitious plans had to be scaled down and eventually, after all the usual legal problems of preserving a line had been ironed out, the Loughborough to Rothley section was designated as a viable proposition.

Loughborough Central is the home of the Great Central Railway, supported by the Main Line Steam Trust Limited. You enter Central Station at a high level from the main road. The large booking-hall is exactly as it was when first built, with varnished wood panelling and

period lamps. I did wonder when I visited the station whether a few plants or flowers would have given a little colour to the wood surrounds, but the whole area is in spick and span condition. There is a long wooden staircase leading down to the platform areas, and on the left of the staircase and part of it, a wooden slide which was used by the porters to move large trunks to and from the platforms in Edwardian and Victorian times. I'll bet children slide down this helpful piece of station equipment if they get the chance. The wood is certainly shiny with wear and age, and just right for a little caper when no one is looking. I am sure I would have been tempted as a youngster.

It is lovely to see a well-preserved canopy and awning over a station platform, and Loughborough has a large glass one with hanging baskets of flowers adding to the overall handsome effect. The island-type station platforms are deceiving in length and can accommodate quite a long train. My guide for the day took me round the small museum which is housed in part of the old lift shaft, put in by British Rail to save the porters having to use the slide for luggage. Thank goodness the slide itself was left intact to register a piece of the station's history. The museum contains a great many items of memorabilia and photographs, including one depicting the building of the station in 1897. In nearly all early photos of railway construction building workers were called navvies, named originally when work was carried out on the navigational canals. Their wages of the time are also noted. There is a well-stocked shop in the main platform building that caters for all ages, and a large café next door serves light meals and snacks on open days. There is also an Information Office and a Ladies' Room which I was able to see, and which has been carefully restored to its Victorian elegance (and why shouldn't a loo be elegant?). The sidings beyond the platforms carry some very unusual coaches including two open saloons built in 1910 in Manchester. The engine-sheds cover a large area, and during my visit seemed to be full of locomotives in a state of refurbishment. The signal-box which controls all the comings and goings of the station is original, and again has been restored from a derelict condition.

There is something rather special about visiting a signal-box. It's a chummy place and I've shared many a cup of tea with a signalman when he's not too busy. The giant levers used for changing the points are always handled with a duster because of the strong leverage required, and in consequence the duster does its own regular polishing of the lever arms. A signalman has to be a fairly powerful fellow in the running of this part of the railway system. He is the decision maker when it comes to the movement of traffic, and is certainly well-disciplined in controlling even a few miles of track. I don't think you would call the Great Central Railway-preserved line a particularly glamorous one, but the hard work and financial resources that have gone into restoring the stations is very considerable, and it has obviously been worthwhile.

Quorn and Woodhouse Station is only a short distance from Loughborough, and is a smaller version of it. It has original mailtrain pick-up and set-down equipment in working order, a light-refreshment-room, shop and picnic area and very importantly a large tarmacked carpark which was once the old goods yard. This station was heavily used in 1944 as a major troop embarkation point for the D-day landings in France. There are designated country walks from the station which you can find out about at the shop.

Three miles on is Rothley, at the moment the southern terminus of the railway. Rothley is roughly the same size as Quorn and Woodhouse, but has a more enclosed atmosphere. The restoration has been carefully carried out to the original Victorian specifications complete with gas-lamps. The flower-beds are also splendid. Rothley is the end of the line at the moment, but preparations are nearing completion to extend the line to a newly built station, Belgrove and Birstall, on the outskirts of Leicester. This will give the Great Central Railway seven and a half miles of railroad and four stations for the public to enjoy. The original Great Central Railway did a great deal to improve travel during the heyday of the railways, and the present company are doing the same thing for this preserved section of the line.

MELDRETH ROAD CROSSING HOUSE

I felt I had to include this even though it is not a station. At one time all level-crossing houses were inhabited by a railway employee who was in charge of the crossing gates. One such house is Meldreth Road, on the main line from London to Cambridge where the gates are now automated. Douglas Fuller was the man in charge here before he retired, and he and his wife Margaret managed to buy the house when it came up for sale at auction. It had been their home for many years when Douglas worked for British Rail. When I visited them they were thrilled that it was now

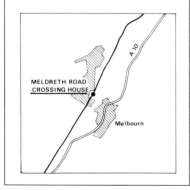

their own home, and were looking forward to carrying out some necessary improvement.

The gardens surrounding this house are most unusual and striking. I have never seen so many flowers and shrubs in one area in my life. Everything is grown from seed, planted and tended by Margaret Fuller and a young man, John Marlar, who has lived with the Fullers for several years. The lawn is also beautifully kept and this complements everything within the gardens, and is complete with rockeries and gravel paths. Although the overall size is not really large you imagine it is because of the amount of plants that are on show.

Visitors are not discouraged, and many people each year visit this miniature horticultural show. Donations are accepted and quite a lot of money is raised for the National Gardens Scheme. People come here from all over the world and bring Margaret Fuller little mementos from their different countries. Margaret is a busy and vibrant lady who deserves the praise that so many people give her.

If you do have time pay the Crossing House a visit, but please take care of this little paradise beside the railway.

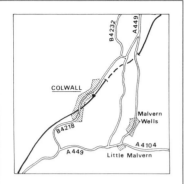

COLWALL

Colwall, a sprawling village to the south-west of the Malvern Hills, is designated as part of an area of outstanding beauty, but in 1984 its railway station was such an eyesore that judges in the Best Kept Village Competition commented adversely on the 'local black spot'.

In 1984 British Rail offered to match any money raised by local Women's Institute groups to improve railway stations in country areas. Colwall WI accepted the challenge to clean up and plant the station platform with flower-beds and shrubs, and a small band of enthusiasts set about raising money through coffee mornings and donations.

From 1968 the station deteriorated into an unmanned single line with a platform strewn with litter and weeds. With encouraging support from the community £250 was raised, British Rail provided a matching £250, and work got under way in the autumn of 1984.

Heavy pick-axe work was carried out by the ladies and a factory developer on adjacent land provided top soil, rocks for edging and a bulldozer to prepare the grass area. Local residents supplied several plants, shrubs and some labour. A grant of £100 from the Countryside Commission and £60 from the local Parish Council swelled the funds and helped to cover the initial purchase of more top-soil, manure, grass turves and trees. British Rail, impressed by the transformation, painted the shelter and bridge in the old Great Western Railway colours of chocolate and cream.

Maintenance of the now attractive station, which provides one of the best views of the Malvern Hills, is divided between a group of volunteers – each one undertaking the weeding and replenishing of specified beds and areas, and a cleaning rota was set up to keep the station tidy. Coffee mornings continue to raise funds for maintenance and the cost of a contractor to mow the grass.

Although the WI still provide the driving force behind the project it could not manage without the active support of the community helpers.

In 1986 Colwall won a Highly Commended certificate in the Best Kept Village Competition, with favourable comments on the now attractive railway station.

Well done ladies – carry on the good work!

The original Colwall Station between Hereford and Malvern in Worcestershire, was opened in 1861 and rebuilt around the turn of the century.

In 1860 engineer Stephen Ballard built Colwall tunnel through the Malvern Hills for the Worcester and Hereford Railway, which lies just north of Colwall. Ballard was born at Malvern Link, and he later settled with his family in the area and became very attached to Colwall. One of his actions was the planting of lime trees from one end of the village to the other.

The downhill gradient of Colwall tunnel was so acute that goods trains had to stop at the station while the guard got out to brake the trucks. As

The fairies have been to Colwall

the train then started the guard would stand on the platform and lever the brakes of the individual trucks with a shunting pole and then finally jump back into his guard's van as it passed him. Until the 1950s all passenger trains were also required to stop at Colwall on their way to Malvern, Worcester, Birmingham and London, and then proceed slowly into the tunnel.

The hardness of the rock delayed the full opening of the line and the tunnel was so troublesome that in 1926 an entirely new one was completed and the old one sealed up, and used as an ammunition store during the Second World War.

Early in the 1900s Colwall became very busy with the farming and fruit-growing industry in Worcestershire. The goods yard was constantly in use and was situated between the station and the station-master's house. Both platforms had a waiting-room, toilets and also a bookstall.

When the various fruit wagons arrived (horse-drawn then) and nearly always at the last minute, to load the boxes of produce on to the Birmingham and London trains, the goodwill of the passengers as well as the station staff was apparent when the travellers used to leave the train and help with the loading in the guard's van. Perhaps the thought behind this was that the sooner they were on board, the sooner they would be on their way. Also of interest was the gate on the down platform with access to the nearby racecourse. During race meetings jockeys and stable lads were housed in 'bothies' (huts) adjacent to the station-master's house.

Although there was gas lighting in the village the station had electricity, and the large amount of lighting on the platforms coupled with the coloured lights of the signals made for a fairyland effect. There was also a well-lit signal-box between the station and the tunnel.

The last station-master at Colwall from 1951 was Mr E. W. Tennant who was very highly thought of by the whole community, but then station-masters were very much a part of the local community. He was a keen gardener, winning several awards, and always made sure the flower-beds, tubs and hanging baskets were bright with flowers. His proudest moment came when the Queen Mother alighted from her train at the station to congratulate him on his wonderful floral display.

The station-master's house is still there, but it is now privately owned and remains a part of Colwall's railway history. The line is now a single track again with only one of the two platforms in use. The original footbridge still spans both platforms and joins up two public footpaths. It is also a good vantage point to see the flower-beds and walled patio garden with its large wooden seat, to rest awhile as they say.

The Great Western Railway were the last owners of the railway before British Rail took over in 1948. It is generally accepted that the hard work of the Cotswold Line Promotion Group played a large part in keeping Colwall Station open when at one point it was in doubt.

An interesting point is found at the next station down the line, Ledbury, where travel agent Gareth Davis has a concession from British Rail to sell tickets. Davis has built a wooden ticket-office and waiting-room, and is shortly erecting a more permanent structure. British Rail is so pleased with the project that it may be repeated at other stations in the area.

DOLAU

Dolau Station, on the Central Wales Line, provides an essential communication link for the small community it serves and that community has responded handsomely.

In June 1983 a group of HOWLTA volunteers decided to undertake a 'one-off' exercise clearing weeds and debris from part of the down platform in preparation for the first locomotive-hauled passenger train (a charter from Llanelli to Llandudno) since the lifting of the ban imposed on locomotives on the Central Wales Line in 1980. Further work took place when it was learned that the Royal Train, conveying the Queen to the Royal Welsh Show, would be passing through Dolau on the 21st July. Out of these events a working group emerged which has met regularly ever since.

The group of volunteers, currently numbering eight – most of whom have been involved in the work since it was started – have done a splendid job of enhancing the station. The platforms have been cleared of weeds and the palings and waiting shelters given a new coat of paint. Rose bushes and trees have been planted and flower tubs and hanging baskets decorate the station. In 1990 a record number of bedding plants – over one thousand – were planted in the flower-beds and a station lamp was installed. It's not surprising Dolau Station has received the Geoffrey Farr Award for community involvement.

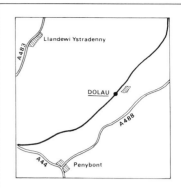

DOLAU
Opened 1864
Central Wales Railway

This railway had a very short independent life, being taken over in 1868 by the London & North Western Railway in order to provide that company with access to South Wales. For many years through-coaches were run from Euston to Swansea via Shrewsbury and the Central Wales line, a roundabout route compared with the Great Western's direct line from Paddington, but indicative of the intense competition between the old railway companies. During both World Wars the line carried heavy freight traffic. Since nationalisation the railway has led a charmed life. Twice it has been formally proposed for closure, in 1962 and 1967, but has been reprieved. Now it seems to have a more assured future, at the cost of minimum facilities at stations and a simplified signalling system. Formerly the line through Dolau had double track, but it was singled in 1965 as part of the conversion of the line to 'basic railway'. The two platforms had low, wooden huts of a standard London & North Western pattern, and there were sidings, signals and a signal-box. Although these have now all gone, at least the skeletal station remains open.

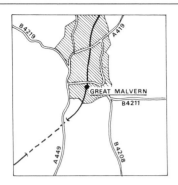

GREAT MALVERN
Line opened in 1860; station completed in 1863
Worcester & Hereford Railway
Listed Grade II

A gem of a station, built in Malvern Hill stone with Bath stone dressings and deliberately created to enhance this spa town, which in 1860 was enjoying great popularity. It is one of very few stations in Britain that was designed as a complete entity, with its approach road, frontage gardens and bridges all in a matching style that, most importantly, also included the Imperial Hotel. The architect for the whole scheme, E. W. Elmslie of the local firm of Elmslie, Franey and Haddon, chose what has been called the Gothic style of Charles VI of France. Unfortunately the delicately proportioned clock turret and slender spirelet were removed in the 1960s, although an appeal has been launched for a replica, which would complete the fine restoration work recently completed following a fire. But the station's chief glory is the series of floral iron capitals on the awning columns, each one different and not cast, but individually beaten and now restored in their original vivid colours.

In its edition of 3rd January 1863 *The Builder* commented on the 'good carving in capitals and elsewhere by W. Forsyth, who has cleverly introduced foliage of the plants in the neighbourhood'

GREAT MALVERN

When you see Great Malvern Station, you feel that it should have something unusual and interesting to offer the railway traveller and when you enter this rather lovely building you are not disappointed, it feels as if you have gone back to the heyday of genteel retirement. Almost without exception every view of the up platform and nearby road bridge (which in fact is listed) is quite marvellous. Lady Foley's tea-room with its tables and chairs on the platform is indicative of a former age. The whole air of the station is one of a conservatory effect, not only because of its hanging baskets but also because of the floral iron capitals on the support columns. On the down platform, the once well-used passageway, under the road into the grounds of the Imperial Hotel (now a girls' school) on the other side of the road bridge, still exists but is not now in use, although the entrance to it in the station still has its old iron gates in place. I suspect this small tunnel was built to make life easy for the station porters who without it would have had a long and arduous walk up the hill and over the bridge to the hotel with travellers' luggage. I wonder whether the passageway was closed when the hotel became a girls' school simply because it had become redundant in the circumstances, or did the school authorities think that any schoolgirl who might be tempted to take the short cut could have been in any danger?

The station staff are justly proud of their buildings and are very happy to show you round. The once-prominent clock turret is again under discussion and hopefully will be reinstalled in the not-too-distant future.

One small point I have to make about the down platform is that I wish a little more thought could have been given to the type of flower-beds that have been made in that area. They really should have been more architecturally in common with the station in general. Behind that down platform is a complex of bungalows, and I suspect the new high brick-built flower-beds were designed to blend in with them and not with the station. However, even with their square lines it's good to have the flower-beds in place.

THE SEVERN VALLEY RAILWAY

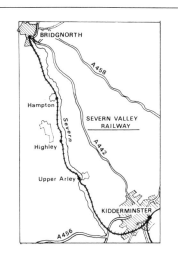

Before I arrived at Kidderminster Town Station, the southern terminus of the Severn Valley Railway, I didn't really know what to expect. I knew it was a station recently built by the Severn Valley Railway Company, but what sort of station was it? A small wooden structure hastily built to give the passengers a jumping-off area for their trip to Bridgnorth, the northern terminus of the Severn Valley Railway? Not a bit of it. Imagine my surprise when I found a station that not only looks very good but also has all the conveniences the travelling public require.

Kidderminster Town Station is a fine building, only six or seven years old, but with the atmosphere of being much older. It was designed from the original plans of the Great Western Railway Station at Ross-on-Wye. You enter through the ticket-hall-cum-waiting-room with its polished woodwork, long upholstered seats, a well-cared-for GWR trolley, and large colourful posters inviting you to visit all the best seaside resorts in the country, as was the custom sixty years ago or more in the heyday of steam railways. You can also enter the station by the King and Castle bar/

Kidderminster Station – the end of the line

69

restaurant where fine and unusual ales are dispensed. Adjoining the bar is the seating and eating area (and presumably another place to await your train). This eating area is at first glance original, but it's a mistake to think that. It is all part of this new building, in fact the whole site was part of the old GWR goods yard for the mainline station next door.

My guide for the couple of hours I was on the premises was Roger Stubbs, who arrived hotfoot from his business in nearby Dudley. Memories came back to me of the wonderful Dudley Hippodrome owned and run by the late Sam Newsome. The Hippodrome played host to every great music hall and pantomime star in the country. I remember seeing a super pantomime there in the late 1950s starring Morecambe and Wise, Stan Stennett, the Canadian vocal quartet Maple Leaf Four, and Mrs Shufflewick.

But I digress – to get back to Roger Stubbs, a charming, enthusiastic and very knowledgeable member of the Severn Valley Railway Company. Roger is very proud of this railway, and he has every right to be. We talked about the fine building we were in, and apparently even the ceiling cornices and slightly larger-than-normal water pipes were meticulously copied from the original plans, not to mention the GWR-patterned carpet specially woven in Kidderminster. (Kidderminster has always been a centre of the carpet industry.) The open concourse to the station has period seats and colourful hanging baskets, which fortunately are once again becoming a familiar sight on many railway stations all over the country. At the farthest end of the platform one very large station signboard has metal letters that have been collected from redundant station signs from all over the country. 'K's from one area, 'A's from another, 'R's from another etc., all exactly the same size. I also found out why the station is called Kidderminster Town. It is only fifty yards from the British Rail Kidderminster Station, a rather small building in

comparison with the SVR 'Town', especially considering it is on the main Birmingham to Worcester line. In the past, when towns boasted two or even three stations, the nearest to the town centre was always called the 'Town', so as the Severn Valley Railway building is approximately fifty yards nearer the town centre than the British Rail one it was quite naturally given the name Kidderminster Town.

Uppermost in the minds of SVR management is to encourage people to use their line to see and discover the surrounding area. In other words it is not a railway just to see steam-engines in action. While in Kidderminster (before journeying on the Severn Valley Railway of course) you have many attractions. There's the Wyre Forest Glades Leisure Centre with a magnificent swimming-pool, and if your stay in the area gives you a chance to visit the Rose Theatre you will certainly enjoy any production you may see there.

However, back to the journey. The first stop on the line from Kidderminster is Bewdley, which was linked to Kidderminster by a loop in 1878 after the Great Western Railway had absorbed the Severn Valley line into their network. The original Severn Valley Railway ran between Hartlebury and Shrewsbury via Bewdley and had been opened in 1862. Bewdley is more than just an attractive station complete with a large amount of period paraphernalia, it is the administrative headquarters of the Severn Valley Railway. Not just another stop on your journey, it is, much to the satisfaction of the SVR, a station that people use to enjoy all the good things that Bewdley is famous for. A Safari and Leisure Park for all the family to enjoy is close at hand, some fine old buildings of architectural interest, and the working museum where you can see demonstrations of the ancient crafts practised in the town, among them rope-making which was a big industry at one time, carried out by the well-known firm of Lowe's (no relation to my dear friend the late Arthur

71

Lowe, at least he never mentioned that he was a rope spinner as well as an actor, but the little rascal could have been keeping it a secret!).

It is now on past Northwood Halt, unless you wish to get out there, in which case it is a request stop, and then you will come to Victoria Bridge over the River Severn, the largest cast-iron clear span in the world when it was built in 1861. This really is a beautiful part of the journey, and once over the bridge it's into a deep cutting and on to the picturesque station of Arley. This station was built in 1862 and has been lovingly restored by the Severn Valley Railway Company. Volunteers rebuilt the decaying platforms with bricks from a station near Bromsgrove. The old track was relaid and a restored signal-box, formerly sited near Whitchurch, was put in and connected to the old-style signalling equipment.

If you have time you should break your journey at Arley, to enjoy a drink and snack at a nearby pub, The Harbour or The Valencia Inn, or stroll along by the river and maybe picnic in the areas designated for your pleasure.

Highley Station was once very important on the original Severn Valley line for the nearby collieries. When preservation started in 1970 the buildings were structurally good, including the signal-box opposite the single platform, but the interiors needed to be repaired. A kiosk has been built from original plans and the surroundings have been landscaped to make Highley a most attractive site. The whole station now looks as it would have done in Edwardian times. It has, with Arley and Kidderminster Town, won awards for Britain's Best Restored Station.

Hampton Loade is a small station but was very important in the early stages of preservation, as it was until 1974 the southern terminus of the railway before steam-hauled services were extended initially to Bewdley and then to Kidderminster. The River Severn is good for fishing in the vicinity so it is popular with fishermen from the Midlands particularly (change at Kidderminster). Many of the refurbishments have been carried out by the station staff at their own expense. The station has a good collection of original photographs of the Severn Valley Railway. This is another station with good adjacent pubs (thirsty people in this area), The Lion stands on one side of the river and The Unicorn on the other. Before getting to Bridgnorth, the northern terminus of the railway, we cross the Oldbury viaduct built originally for double track to take the abortive scheme of a railway from Wolverhampton to Bridgnorth. The latter was the birthplace of the preservation scheme for the railway. North of Bridgnorth is the famous Ironbridge Gorge Museum Trust where a small original section of the railway of the Severn Valley line still exists, but some of the rest has been built on, so from Bridgnorth to Ironbridge it is unlikely to be reinstated. South of Bridgnorth, after closure by British Rail in 1963, it was saved at the eleventh hour by the preservationists who then set to work. Bridgnorth Station has a proper refreshment-room called The Railwayman's Arms, a smart bookshop and extended platforms. Behind Platform 2 is the locomotive works, where you will see all the hard work in progress, typical of an engineering centre for locomotive servicing and repairs.

Together with several other preserved lines the Severn Valley is worth returning to – it's impossible to take it all in the first time round.

GOBOWEN

If you were an army serviceman in the Second World War the chances are you would have changed at this station for Oswestry which was a huge intake military camp.

Gobowen has been superbly refurbished by the Railway Heritage Trust, and is a marvellous example of the partnership between British Rail and the Trust.

GOBOWEN
Opened 1848
Shrewsbury & Chester
Railway
Listed Grade II

In architectural terms Gobowen is a delight, although sadly its unique Florentine charm, complete with campanile-like turret, for a number of years languished in sore disrepair until local organisations campaigned for its restoration. The work was completed in 1989, winning a Railway Heritage Award. Originally the station was the junction for Oswestry and the Cambrian line to mid-Wales, and the Great Western added the platform awnings and the building on the up side. Why such a perfect little station was built here, in a village with little else of interest, remains something of a mystery.

The results of the Railway Heritage Trust's renovation

73

RAILWAY HERITAGE TRUST
by Sir William McAlpine

As the owner of well over one thousand listed buildings and structures in the United Kingdom, British Rail is justifiably proud of its rich heritage. One of the many ways in which this responsibility has been acknowledged was the initiative to set up in 1985 an independent organisation – the Railway Heritage Trust – and by providing financial support of some £1m each year since.

As Chairman of the Trust, therefore, I welcome the publication of this book which illustrates the results of some of the continual efforts being made to enhance the railway heritage and to improve public awareness, and consequently the enjoyment, of railway stations and structures.

During our five years in existence the Trust has supported 205 renovation schemes throughout British Rail with grants amounting to £10m, of which £4.9m was contributed from non-British Rail sources. The geographical and physical spread of these schemes spanned the whole country and ranged in size from the mighty Ribblehead Viaduct on the Settle to Carlisle route to the modest restoration of the station clock on the concourse at Brighton Station.

Included in the schemes which benefited from funding were the stations at Shrewsbury, Gobowen, Aylesford, Stowmarket, Great Malvern, Bristol Temple Meads, Liverpool Street, Paddington and Invergordon. Bridges and viaducts also feature prominently in receiving grants for work associated with the Forth Bridge, Glenfinnan Viaduct, Stockport Viaduct and Runcorn Bridge.

In addition to the provision of financial support for restoration schemes, the Trust assists British Rail in identifying alternative uses for redundant buildings and structures. In this catalytic role, ownership of viaducts has been passed to Local Authorities or interested parties and Trusts for conversion to cycleways, walkways and interpretative sites. Examples of these can be found at Smardale Gill in Cumbria and Dundee and Largo in Scotland.

Although a great deal has been achieved in improving many railway heritage sites, the work yet to be done is considerable. Nevertheless five years of successful operation of the Railway Heritage Trust encourages me to look to the challenge of the future with optimism.

SOUTH

IM TAKING AN
EARLY HOLIDAY COS
i KNOW SUMMER
COMES SOONEST IN THE SOUTH
SOUTHERN RAILWAY

BASINGSTOKE
Opened 1839
London & Southampton
Railway

The original station, designed by
Sir William Tite, rapidly outgrew
its capacity. Despite alterations
and additions over the years it
became a notorious bottleneck for
trains, with only two
through-platforms, but it was
not until 1903–4 that the London
& South Western completely
rebuilt the place, designing an
entirely new layout and
increasing the through-platforms
to four. More recently the station
has been restored and
modernised by British Rail,
transforming the formerly drab
red-brick exterior and landscaping
the approach, to such effect that
the station won a Railway
Heritage Award in 1988.

The success of Business
Community involvement at
Basingstoke

BASINGSTOKE

When you arrive at Basingstoke Station you cannot help but see the signs for 'Provident Life'. You may think this is just an ordinary advertising campaign, but in fact Provident Life Assurance Consultants have played a big part in conjunction with British Rail in the landscaping of flowerbeds, on the platforms and in the whole approach to the station forecourt.

This is a good example of community business partnership which will hopefully increase elsewhere on the rail network, since it benefits everybody. The businesses involved are looked upon by potential customers with a degree of goodwill, and residents feel that something has been put back into the community. Travellers certainly experience the benefits of a bright and well-cared-for station.

Basingstoke is and always has been a good centre of communication, accessible to Winchester and Southampton to the south, Reading and Newbury to the north and Guildford and London to the east. It certainly appears to be the crossroads between the West Country and the Metropolis.

It has had some form of settlement since the year 7000 BC and various cultures have left their mark, including the Neolithic man, Bronze Age people, Celts, Romans, Saxons, Danes and Normans. It became a thriving market town, and at one time it was possible to move goods all the way to London on the Basingstoke and Wey Canal which was opened in 1794, which after many years of closure has now been completely cleared and reopened for navigation. This has been a huge undertaking but a thoroughly worthwhile project.

The railway from London to the south via Basingstoke was opened in 1839 and other rail routes into the town followed. Businesses were attracted to the area and several very large companies are now based there, including the Automobile Association.

My first introduction to the town was in 1948 when I was working at Burberry's store in London's Haymarket, and their factory and warehouse was in Basingstoke. It had been rebuilt after a disastrous fire there in 1905. A Burberry raincoat in my time was a legend, and customers would hang on to them as long as they could with frequent reproofing of the garment which was done at another factory in Reading. George Formby filmed *He Snoops to Conquer* in the town and Will Hay's *Oh Mr Porter* was filmed on the disused Basingstoke to Alton line. More recently it has been used, I suspect, as a lucky omen, by comedy writer Ray Cooney, who has used 'Basingstoke' in some of his very successful plays, *There Goes the Bride* and *Run For Your Wife* amongst them. I have appeared in both these productions and all the actors concerned give Ray a wry smile when it comes to the 'Basingstoke' lines.

Perhaps Basingstoke and similar stations like it should be used as a model for community and industry involvement with British Rail, in the restoration and refurbishment of station buildings.

LIPHOOK

Liphook is on the London Waterloo to Portsmouth line. It is very easy to ignore this little station as you rush through it on your journey south, unless of course you are getting on or off there. There is nothing particularly interesting about it on the platform side, although it once had attractive hanging baskets and flower-beds, which I suspect was due to members of the staff who are no longer in service there. The small outside entrance to the station, however, has been refurbished to its original design, and is very pleasing to the eye.

Liphook is a pleasant Hampshire township, not very big but with some fine houses and a famous seventeenth-century coaching inn, The Royal Anchor Hotel. Nearby are the Bohunt Gardens of the Worldwild Fund for Nature, and at Hollycombe House there is an interesting collection of steam-powered fairground machinery, plus a two-foot-gauge mini-railway.

You could start your visit at Liphook's British Rail station and end it on the Hollycombe Railway, you won't be disappointed.

LIPHOOK
Opened 1859
Portsmouth Railway

Liphook stands on the line from Godalming to Havant. The Portsmouth Railway was built as a speculative venture by the great Victorian railway contractor Thomas Brassey as a direct line from London to Portsmouth, for sale to the highest bidder – of which the two most obvious were the rival London & South Western and London Brighton & South Coast railways. The former company acquired it in 1859, six months after it was opened, but not before its construction had sparked off a row between the two railways, that led to the so-called 'Battle of Havant' when both companies removed rails and blocked the line to prevent the passage of each other's trains, resulting in legal proceedings. Liphook Station largely retains its original symmetrical design, which was common to Witley, Haslemere, Liss and Rowlands Castle on the same line, and was repeated elsewhere.

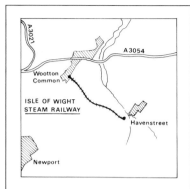

ISLE OF WIGHT STEAM RAILWAY

I don't think it would be an exaggeration to say that millions of people have stood on the promenade at Southsea in Hampshire and looked across the Solent water with longing and some excitement at the little island on the other side. I know I have.

Your visit to the Isle of Wight, whether it be for a day or a fortnight's annual holiday, begins at the ferry terminal at Portsmouth, a short distance away from Southsea. In the past large passenger ferries carried you to the island rather more slowly than the new catamarans now used on the journey, but at least with the ferry you had time for a cup of tea or a beer and a chat with fellow travellers, some of whom you might exchange holiday addresses with. It was all part of your vacation. The excited chatter of youngsters and the grown-ups talking about 'going abroad', even before you had left Portsmouth Harbour would be the same at anytime.

If you are making for Ryde as a passenger traveller, or taking your car to Fishbourne, the car ferry terminus on the island, or on the Lymington to Yarmouth route, or Southampton to Cowes, you soon start picking out landmarks on the way. Ryde church spire for instance towering above the town, or Wootton Creek just round the corner from Osborne House, Queen Victoria's lovely residence where she spent much of her time after her beloved Albert died.

I discovered the Isle of Wight for the first time in 1964 when I appeared in a Summer Show there at Sandown, and I've been discovering it ever since. There are so many delightful places to stay at and visit on the island. When you land at Ryde Pier, only basically a short journey from Portsmouth, you have left behind all memories of the mainland, even though on a clear day you can still see it. As with most islands, once you are on it you really do forget the hustle and bustle of everyday pressures that we all have to contend with in our normal (some of it abnormal) lives. A slower pace overtakes you, and it's nearly always sunny, at least it seems sunnier there than anywhere else.

The railway station at Ryde Pierhead has only been slightly modernised since the early days of the island railway system. You can now only travel by British Rail from Ryde to Shanklin via St John's and Brading, but a new junction is being built at Smallbrook to connect you with the Isle of Wight Steam Railway.

In the 1860s and 1870s, at the beginning of rail communications on the island, there were several different operating companies. The Isle of Wight Railway, Isle of Wight Central Railway, The London, Brighton and South Coast Railway, jointly with The London and South Western Railway, and the Freshwater, Yarmouth and Newport Railway. Railways criss-crossed the towns and countryside, from Ryde to Newport, Ventnor to Cowes, Bembridge to Freshwater. Although few of the companies did well financially, by 1900 the island had become tremendously popular as a holiday resort. 'Something for everyone on this little piece of land surrounded by water' someone once said to me, and they're right. There is Ventnor, the island's French Riviera, Sandown and Shanklin for the children, Bembridge, Yarmouth and Cowes for sailing, and the attraction of places like Black Gang Chine, the historical Carisbrooke Castle and Osborne House which I've already mentioned, still in its original state internally and externally for visitors to enjoy. Nowadays the island caters for teenagers, with resident Disco Clubs, and there are Holiday Camp sites in abundance, but it has never forgotten how to welcome Mum and Dad, many of whom have been going there since they themselves were youngsters.

One of the biggest attractions for all age groups is the Isle of Wight Steam Railway, whose headquarters are at Haven Street Station which was part of the original Ryde to Newport line. By 1923 when the Isle of Wight railways were taken over by the Southern Railway in the big four grouping, it was realised that the previous companies had been lacking in investment and the Southern had to spend a good deal of money on new track, stations and signalling equipment, but it all seemed worthwhile because the holidaymakers were still coming to the island in their thousands. Everything was fine until just after the Second World War when in the 1950s the motor-car came to the Isle of Wight in a big way and the railways became far less profitable. British Rail, then the owners, started making plans for closure and by 1966 the whole system was closed down apart from the section from Ryde to Shanklin, which was modernised and is now run with ex-London Underground trains.

It was about the time of the closures that a group of people formed a new Isle of Wight Railway Company and were able to make plans for the preservation of a small section of one of the lines from Haven Street to Wootton. The volunteer group had to purchase the track from British Rail in 1971 as the existing rails all over the island were being removed with great speed, and the hard work didn't end there. Weeding the track, refurbishing the main station and some of the original island engines and rolling-stock was all carried out by the volunteers who gave up their weekends and holidays and worked very long hours to obtain their objective. It was 1978 before the company received their Light Railway Order which enabled them to run regular passenger services.

Although Haven Street was completely rebuilt in 1926, and looks nothing like the rather plain little building of 1900, the present main structure is well-proportioned in brick and timber, and painted in the colours of the Southern Railway. There is a garden at either end, one leading down to the new refreshment-room and small kiddies' play area. On the opposite side of the station platform is yet another small garden with comfortable seats, and next to it is the Society's shop and museum with its comprehensive range of artifacts from the original island railways. Farther to the right is the very large engine-shed and workshop. The museum building dates back to 1886 and was once part of the village gas-works. The large water tower comes from the old station at Newport. The original name of the village was Hethenstrete, meaning a road constructed by heathens. The change in the name came about because rather naturally the villagers didn't like to be known as heathens, and who can blame them. The short journey to the other Isle of Wight Steam Railway station at Wootton, passes through some lovely scenery, but then you might expect that on the island. Wootton is typical of a country halt and was built by the new company just on the other side of the original station. It has the most delightful signal-box which looks almost like a

80

doll's-house, surrounded by a miniature garden.

Now we come to the most exciting development since the Isle of Wight Steam Railway was opened some years ago: the extension from Haven Street to Ashey and Smallbrook Junction which will give the railway a direct link with British Rail trains from Ryde. This link has always been in the minds of the Isle of Wight Steam Railway Company and with the co-operation and help of British Rail the project is about to materialise. British Rail are building the junction station, and the Isle of Wight Steam Railway are relaying the trackbed and track. A lot of the track has come from the section of the up-line at Brading, which has not been used for some time on the Ryde/Shanklin line as single line operating is quite adequate now at Brading. Some of the station buildings may also be removed and will be re-erected at Smallbrook. The clearing of the original trackbed, levelling, and the laying of hundreds and hundreds of tons of ballast ready for the track-laying itself has taken the volunteer workers hours of their spare time, some of it at night with big arc lamps for illumination. All the new signalling equipment and signals have to be provided for the line but, as I've been told, it will all have been worth it when the time comes for the official opening, in 1991. It will then give people the chance to travel directly to Ashey, Haven Street and Wootton from Ryde, changing at Smallbrook, and of course you'll be able to travel from the village of Wootton to Ryde in the opposite direction giving that part of the island direct communication again with the town of Ryde and, combined with the ferry, a link with London.

I wonder if that original small group of railway preservationists ever visualised that it would eventually be possible for people to travel again from Wootton to London's Waterloo with just two changes, but then the determination of those original volunteers and their successors is what the preserved railway companies are all about.

81

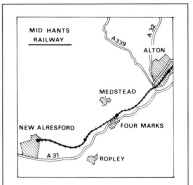

THE MID-HANTS RAILWAY
'THE WATERCRESS LINE'

'Watercress and Arlott.' It sounds like a refined music-hall double act or a summer appetiser to a main course. Those words were said to me by someone when we were talking about Alresford, 'When I think of that lovely Hampshire market town I always think of watercress and Arlott, and the Mid-Hants Railway.'

The famous watercress beds that were a feature of the town certainly played their part in Alresford's busy market trade and produced revenue for the railway when the delicious plant was sent all over the country. I guessed the Arlott my acquaintance was talking about was broadcaster John Arlott. John's radio commentaries and his very distinctive voice in describing so many great cricket occasions is I believe unique in the annals of radio. Before his cricket broadcasting days he was a poetry reader for the Home and the World Service programmes of the BBC. John is a wine connoisseur, a lover of good books and sporting prints, and through my personal contact with him one of the gentlest of men you could wish to meet. A real son of Hampshire since his early childhood in Basingstoke and a long-time resident of Alresford before he moved to the little island of Alderney a few years ago.

Present-day Alresford, however, is very definitely famous as the head-quarters of the Mid-Hants Railway. It is part of the line that was originally built when the south-western area was expanding in the heyday of rail transport. By 1861 the London and South Western Railway reached from London in all directions, including Southampton to cope with the increasing ocean-liner trade. It was at this time that the newly formed Alton, Alresford and Winchester Railway Company was given parliamentary permission to lay down a line for this area of Hampshire. The line was opened in 1865 and renamed the Mid-Hants Railway Company. The London and South Western operated the actual trains, but eventually in the 1880s took over complete control of the Mid-Hants Railway. Apart from linking the small towns of the area it gave the London and South Western Railways a relief line to Winchester from London and vice versa. In fact the line was heavily used for troop movements to Southampton from nearby Aldershot and surrounding areas of Army depots during the First World War. It was similarly used during the Second World War and the Suez crisis of 1956.

In 1923 the London and South Western Railways became part of the Southern Railway. By the 1930s passenger and freight traffic had become much less due to the increase in road transport. However, the line was still popular with local commuters and those who wished to travel further afield, even as far as Southampton, but it had developed into much more of a branch line. Towards the end of the 1950s diesel trains were introduced, and with people starting to live farther and farther away from London large increases occurred in the number of passengers using the line to make connections with commuter trains at Alton. Despite this, in

the mid 1960s station staff were reduced and the line received its share of cuts, and all the stations on the branch, with the exception of Alresford, became unmanned. After many on-off decisions the whole line was eventually closed by British Rail in 1973.

At this point the first negotiations by a preservation society started to bear fruit and although the track from Winchester to Alresford had been lifted, plans to save the rest of the line as far as Alton now seemed possible. As with other preserved railways, the hard work and determination to succeed had only just begun, but it was a start. Money was sought through share issues, British Rail was paid off, and the Society members began the task of restoration. The 1980s was a decade of feverish activity and the renamed (and original) Mid-Hants Railway was really on its way.

Once you have passed the residential area just outside Alton the journey to Alresford in a south-westerly direction is very much a rural one. Travelling on a high embankment for two or three miles you can see stretches of the Hampshire countryside not normally visible. Passing the village of Chawton, which was once the home of Jane Austen, the first station down the line is Medstead and Four Marks. Originally named Medstead, the station was a mile away from the village, which was not uncommon in the early days of rail pioneering. Four Marks was added to the name in the late 1930s to include the growing development of that village very close to the station. After the line was finally closed by British Rail in 1973 Medstead and Four Marks was badly vandalised and hardly

83

recognisable. Once the line was preserved, Society members, all volunteers, spent a lot of time and much labour restoring it to its original design.

The Mid-Hants Railway Company has not only preserved part of a famous line, it has also played a big part in creating the opportunity to preserve some of this country's vintage omnibuses. The Mid-Hants Railway offered the Working Omnibus Museum a home after the Society was forced to move from its original base. It was only the dedication of a few private bus owners that saved the Society from extinction and preserved many of the buses which are just as much a part of our transport history as the railways. The Mid-Hants Railway offered the Medstead and Four Marks' derelict coal yard as a permanent home for the buses and ever since the Society has been hard at work developing the site to create not only a replica of a 1940–50s country bus garage but also a shop and a museum detailing the story of vehicles from all over the country. Some of the buses are already operating for passengers at certain times of the year.

Now on with the journey to Alresford and the next stop after Medstead and Four Marks is Ropley. This is a fine station, up to main line standards, with offices and residential accommodation. Again the village is a mile away from the station. Ropley is painted in the colours of the London and South Western Railway and the famous topiary on the station has been restored. In 1981 it won a Best Preserved Station Award. Alongside the down-line is the railway's locomotive shed where repairs are carried out and this work can be viewed by visitors to the station.

On we go to the headquarters of the Mid-Hants Railway, Alresford and the end of the line. The watercress area from which the line gets its name is well in evidence before you reach the station. The buildings at Alresford have changed very little since its original construction in the 1860s but they are now painted in the colours of the Southern Railway. More space was required for a shop after preservation took place so the Mid-Hants Railway bought and re-erected the small station building from Lyme Regis, which was closed in 1965, for this purpose. The station has a very good front entrance and impressively redesigned concourse. It will remain the headquarters and terminus of this railway company as the rest of the line to Winchester Junction can never be restored. The land has been built on, at one point accommodating part of the M3 motorway, but the ten-mile journey between Alton and Alresford and vice versa in a train headed by one of their fine collection of refurbished engines is very pleasant indeed.

Like other preserved railways the Mid-Hants Railway has many special days for people to enjoy, such as Santa specials for the children during the Christmas period and Thomas the Tank Engine weekends.

On Sunday, 16th September, 1990, one of these special days for the Mid-Hants Railway was 'War on the Line' a day of nostalgia marking the fiftieth anniversary of the Battle of Britain. I was invited down to judge the stations for the best overall atmosphere of wartime Britain and I found the enthusiasm of the staff and visitors marvellous.

I arrived at Alresford, and after parking my car I was confronted by a display of vintage small cars – many Austin Sevens, and an Auster

Ropley Station

reconnaissance aeroplane of the 1940s period. The entrance to the station was sandbagged and manned by Military Police and a WAAF, an ATS girl and a host of people, including two newspaper reporters, waiting to take photographs of my 'arrest'. I had by this time put on my *Dad's Army* white helmet to make everything authentic. Mainwaring and his Home Guard mob never made me feel too welcome in their company, but at least they never actually arrested me!

The Military Police having had their fun, and the Press satisfied, I was released to enjoy a warming and welcome cup of coffee administered by Managing Director Ian Dean and was ready for the off. In the company of Robin Higgs, Chairman of Mid-Hants Railway and his wife Heather we left Alresford Station for the uninterrupted journey to Alton, where we began our judging. Here we met volunteer staff, dressed in 1940s costume who amongst other things were selling period jam sandwiches. (At least it wasn't beetroot jam that we actually ate during the war!) Music of the period was playing along with sounds of air-raid sirens and bombers droning through the skies. I remember it well! We also saw a couple of Army vehicles from the D-day Exhibition at Southsea, which is worth a visit if you are in the Portsmouth area. Then leaving Alton we made the return journey, setting out for Four Marks, and it was then that I was invited to ride on the footplate of the engine, the very large and powerful Franklin D. Roosevelt. This beautifully restored engine was discovered in a terrible condition in Greece. It had, along with other American locomotives, been used during the Second World War to pull military trains in overseas combat areas. It was the first time I had ridden in a steam-engine cab, and it really gave me a wonderful view of the surrounding countryside.

After a long climb we stopped at Medstead and Four Marks for our judging, and here again the atmosphere was marvellous. Station signs had been blocked out as in wartime, and there were sandbags round the entrances. Notices everywhere told us that 'Careless talk costs lives' and that we should all 'Dig for Victory'. An unexploded bomb was embedded in the platform embankment which gave the whole effect great credulity.

Now to Ropley, and it was really buzzing. Special notices, one appertaining to *Dad's Army* and an air-raid shelter gave it an authentic wartime look. American and British soldiers were in abundance with many vehicles of both nations assembled in the normal picnic area adjoining the station. From my vantage point in the engine cab I was able to see all the various plots of land beside and around the stations that are owned by the company. This land, all freehold, will be used to enrich the future of the Mid-Hants Railway and there seems no doubt in the minds of the Company Directors and staff that it will all happen in due course.

Back to Alresford, and after looking round at the many inventive ideas here towards this 'War on the Line' day, it was time to decide which station had the vote. How difficult to decide, everyone had done so well, but we thought that Ropley had won by a short helmet. My Air Raid Warden's helmet from my *Dad's Army* days had done stirling work but was, at the end of a long day, feeling decidedly heavier than it had done at the outset of what turned out to be a very enjoyable event.

The line has seen its fair share of filming both for the large and small screens, and recently it was used as a location for the film *Bullseye*, directed by Michael Winner and starring Michael Caine and Roger Moore.

READING

Reading Station has the same historic railway links as Paddington and Bristol, as the line from London to Somerset (now called Avon) was Brunel's first wide-gauge main line. Reading Station has recently been refurbished and now has a modern shopping square within the building, and apart from the platforms would be hardly recognisable to someone who hasn't visited the station for several years. Apart from its main line significance Reading now has a through branch line to Gatwick Airport via Guildford.

Reading was also once the home of Huntley and Palmer biscuits, known worldwide for its famous 'cream crackers' ('no home should be without them' they used to say). The BBC used to stage *Workers' Playtime* shows from the factory, live performances which started during the war years to boost morale. I took part in one at the end of the 1950s. Practically every performer at one time or another would wait for the news headlines at 12.30 p.m. followed by the compère's unforgettable and frightening words 'Ladies and Gentlemen – from a factory somewhere in Britain – WORKERS' PLAYTIME!' Of course after the war the compère was allowed to mention the factory in question. Reading gaol gained its notoriety when playwright Oscar Wilde was sent there after his famous trial concerning his alliance with 'Bosey' the son of Lord Alfred Douglas and it was at Reading Station that Lawrence of Arabia lost or had stolen (the circumstances are not quite clear) most of the draft copy of *The Seven Pillars of Wisdom*, the account of his life and service in the Arab world. As Lawrence had already thrown away his original notes he had to start again from memory. *The Seven Pillars of Wisdom* was published as a limited edition in 1926 at the then princely sum of £30. It was republished in 1927 in standard form with the title *Revolt in the Desert*.

If you do have occasion to use Reading Station try also to spare some time to look at the marvellous refurbished clock tower which overlooks the station forecourt.

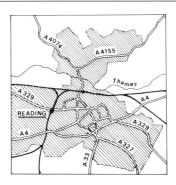

READING
Opened 1840
Great Western Railway
Listed Grade II

For most of the last century Reading Station was a byword for inconvenience and delay. It was one of a number designed by I. K. Brunel with separate 'up' and 'down' platforms on the same side of the line, instead of opposite each other in the more usual manner. Brunel said the arrangement prevented passengers boarding a train going in the wrong direction and avoided their having to cross the line, but in reality these 'one-sided' stations only created problems when trains had to cross each other's paths to get in and out. As each platform had a full range of buildings and facilities, in effect forming two separate stations, there was also the unnecessary expense of having to provide two of everything. Later on a wooden connecting platform was built, but it did little to help. Even so, it was 1896–7 before the GWR built another station, retaining the striking Italianate building with its turret that dates from about 1870. It is now listed and has been incorporated in the new station and shopping mall development recently opened by Her Majesty the Queen.

DENMARK HILL
Opened 1866
London Brighton & South
Coast Railway
Listed Grade II

Denmark Hill Station was one of
the first of a number built in a
distinctive style that marked this
company's medium-sized
stations for the next twenty
years or so. Its size and opulent
appearance reflected the
prosperous suburban community
it served. That community's
successors came to the rescue
after a serious fire in 1980 when
the station was under threat of
demolition. Local organisations
made major contributions
towards restoration, including
Bruce's Brewery which occupied
part of the former booking-hall as
an attractive pub. More recently
the platforms have been
restored to match the entrance
building, with aid from the Railway
Heritage Trust, complete with
period lamps and fittings.

The splendid pub conversion at
Denmark Hill

DENMARK HILL

Denmark Hill Station in south London is quite unusual in that it was
rebuilt after a serious fire in the 1980s and is now part-station, part-very
impressive pub. At ground level the pub is a major part of the building,
and the station entrance and booking-hall a lesser part, but the whole is
certainly a credit to partnership rebuilding by British Rail and the brewery. The interior of the pub is almost dominated by a superb old station
clock and it is worth indulging in a glass of ale and a bite to eat here. In
the summer attractive tables and chairs are outside for your added
pleasure.

ELMSTEAD WOODS

This station is one of many in what has always been a fairly prosperous area of suburbia in south-east England. It was opened in July 1904 and was then called just Elmstead, the 'Woods' being added in 1908. As in suburbia generally, the expansion in housing development in the London Borough of Bromley of which Elmstead is now a part, really took off in the 1920s and 30s and continued after the Second World War, and no wonder. A good train service into London, and within easy access to the Kent countryside or Thanet coast, made it a very desirable place to be, and it still is.

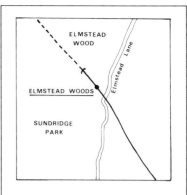

After the management agreement between the London Chatham and Dover Railway with the South Eastern to operate jointly as the South Eastern and Chatham Railway, expansion took place on this line including the building of a second Chislehurst tunnel in 1905 to take extra tracks for the increasing amount of traffic.

Elmstead Woods Station is situated very near to the southern end of the tunnel, and it was said that the wealthy season-ticket holders who lived in the area contributed much financially to the building of it. It became the Southern Railway when they took over ownership in 1923.

Today the station has lost part of its original exterior canopy but it is still a listed building and has had little alteration made to it since it was enlarged in 1901. Peter Phelps, the leading railman and booking-clerk at the station, has given much of his spare time to making the whole area really attractive. There are flower-beds on all the platforms, hanging baskets, and a brightly planted old-fashioned wooden wheelbarrow (the sort Dad and Grandpa used to push round the garden with much puffing and blowing). This is a real garden station. Peter with the help of a colleague does all the planting and subsequent care of the flowers and their hard work has been rewarded with the Borough of Bromley's 'Best Kept Station' annual awards' scheme. Incidentally Bromley is very much involved in the protection and care of the environment in their borough.

Peter Phelps' handiwork at Elmstead Woods Station

There was one mishap to the plants not so long ago. When the platforms were sprayed with weed killer, which is done at night, a lot of the spray got on to the flower-beds. I am sure if Peter could have got hold of the culprits they would have had the sharp end of his tongue. Undeterred he replanted the affected areas and I would advise further thoughts of weed killing by railway linesmen should be abandoned if they value their well-being!

British Rail are aware of Peter's efforts and in fact in co-operation with Bromley Council yet another flower-bed will probably come into existence fairly soon.

Railway stations need people like Peter, and I suggest he should be given the station when he retires instead of the proverbial watch so he can continue to give enjoyment to the customers at Elmstead Woods with his floral displays.

EDEN PARK

In the early 1880s one of the railway lines running from London to the south-east passed through the same area of Kent as Elmstead Woods. A short branch line was proposed to run to Eden Park, West Wickham and Hayes, from Elmers End, one of the stations on this line. The area around these three stations was quiet, with just a handful of rather grand houses, but nevertheless it was thought that eventually it would develop as other areas in the vicinity were starting to do. An ambitious plan was suggested to even go beyond Hayes, but this never came to fruition. In any case it was already surrounded by other lines in and out of London and the coast, and a link up with them seemed unnecessary.

The area in question has certainly developed, but a large amount of 'green' land can still be seen. The building of the branch line was slow due to the landowners making difficulties over the use of their property for the route it was to take. These difficulties were obviously overcome and the line opened at the end of May 1882.

A company called the West Wickham and Hayes Railway made the first proposals for the building of the branch in 1880 but the company was taken over by the South Eastern Railway in 1881 and they designed, built and ran the line. They later became the South Eastern and Chatham Railway. The three stations on the branch were all built in the typical South Eastern style, using wood cladding, but only one of them, Eden Park, is still more-or-less the same today, although it is more than just a railway station.

Leading railwayman Raymond Ashburn and his staff have made the station into one of the happiest and most welcome in the south-east. Flowers are in great evidence, grown by the staff themselves and some by the passengers who use the station, and there is a pond in the middle of the gardens filled with water lilies. The buildings are graffiti-free and regular painting of certain parts has brought the whole station to the notice of passing committees and other societies. Raymond Ashburn was an engine-driver before he came to Eden Park. He had to retire from driving when he was stabbed in the eye, but his enthusiasm and loyalty to the railways has never diminished. The station house, which is rather like a large, timbered fishing village residence, was built on the up-side of the line, and the down-side is reached by a pedestrian tunnel under the track. The waiting-room has a goodly supply of magazines, again supplied by the staff and passengers. While railway station staff are allowed to 'staff' as they are here and at a few other places, British Rail can be assured that at least in some instances they have the most important link between running a railway and its passengers, the station personnel.

RAVENSBOURNE

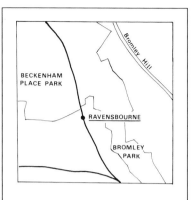

It's a long way from the Seychelles in the Indian Ocean to Ravensbourne in the London Borough of Bromley but to one of their sons it has been a challenge.

Ernest Chang Pin-Tive, a baker in the Seychelles before coming to England, is senior railman at Ravensbourne Station and this friendly man from across the seas has transformed the station entrance into an oasis of colour with a profusion of small hanging baskets, tubs and a large flower-bed bursting with plants. All this is in quite a small area adjoining the booking-hall, and I defy anyone not to have a smile on their face when they arrive to catch their train, even on a Monday morning.

The entrance is in part of the rebuilt station, which was completed in 1987 after a serious fire, of which arson was thought to be the cause. Thanks to the prompt action of the fire brigade the fire did not affect the platform area so seriously and the original building remained intact. The rebuilt area blends in well with the rural surroundings of the station, which is accessible only by an unmade road which divides it from a park and woods which are often used by mounted policemen and women exercising their horses.

The original station at Ravensbourne was opened in 1892 and is on the Catford Loop to Bromley South line and the Kent coast from London which was operated by the London, Chatham and Dover Railway. This company entered into a joint management arrangement with the South Eastern Railway and between them they covered the whole of this area at the end of the last century. The increase in rail traffic went ahead at quite a pace, just as it had on the nearby line from London to Elmstead Woods and beyond. In 1923 it all became part of the Southern Railway.

Ravensbourne Station, like several others in the area, Beckenham Junction, Sundridge Park and Bromley North, has won various prizes in the Best Kept Station category, and as Chang says, 'This is my station so I have to take some pride in it. I grow flowers to plant here, and I want to keep the place clean and tidy. Funnily enough, at home I leave the gardening to my wife.'

Finally let us say the Seychelles' loss is Ravensbourne's gain.

The Seychelles influence at Ravensbourne

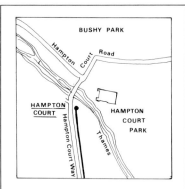

HAMPTON COURT
Opened 1849
London & South Western
Railway
Listed Grade II

The station here was designed by the notable Victorian architect Sir William Tite, who for many years worked for the London & South Western and other railways, but is probably best known for rebuilding the Royal Exchange in the City of London. Although the platforms have been extended, the main building remains much as it was built, with strong Tudor features possibly intended to acknowledge the close proximity of Hampton Court Palace. At one time there was a charming little goods shed behind the station, built to match, with a steep roof and prominent buttresses, but unfortunately it has been demolished.

Hampton Court Station ready to welcome the Royal visitor, but this time not Henry VIII

HAMPTON COURT

It is rumoured that great changes are about to take place at Hampton Court Station. Plans have been suggested to turn the listed station building into a museum with some small retail businesses but this can only happen if and when the development includes an extension to the platforms and a new separate entrance to the station for the travelling public.

I remember going to Hampton Court Palace in 1948 with a girlfriend. We went into the famous maze and both immediately got lost. I think it was about an hour later when we met up again. I felt so stupid repeating, 'Excuse me, is this the way out?'

I hadn't been back to Hampton Court until I visited the Flower Festival there in 1990, which was sponsored by Network South East/British Rail and was opened by the Princess Royal in the usual charming way.

The palace of Hampton Court, beside the River Thames upstream from Kingston, was originally intended to be the sumptuous home of Cardinal Wolsey, but when Henry VIII cast his beady eye on it Wolsey had no option but to give it up to his royal master. Apart from the many beautiful things that can be seen in the palace, there is a 'real' indoor tennis court, once used by Henry VIII and still in use today.

As far as the station is concerned though, it is a listed building that should be preserved in the most practical way possible. It does have a history of its own, it has been used by royalty visiting the palace and grounds, and it can only enhance this area of the Thames Waterway.

VAUXHALL

When you walk into the tunnel entrance to Vauxhall Station, which is just half a mile west of the Houses of Parliament, you might think that you're walking into a huge psychedelic disco without music. The unusual patterns that you see on the walls, which replaced the bare brick when the station was recently renovated, go through a series of light pattern changes, depending on where you stand. Don't ask me how standing on certain paving slabs can do this (it is obviously an electronic device which is beyond my ken), I just enjoyed watching the effects.

Vauxhall Station is sometimes overflowing with travellers. For about five days in August every year, and at a few other select times in the summer months, ladies and gentlemen using the station on these occasions have only one topic of conversation and one aim in mind. The talk is of cricket, and their aim is to get to the Oval cricket ground, a ten-minute walk down the road, as quickly as possible. The Oval is the headquarters of the Surrey County Cricket Club and traditionally the venue for the final Test Match between England and the season's visiting tourists. I would have liked to have been a fly on the wall in 1938 when the crowds were returning to the station after watching the great England batsman, the late Len Hutton, score his record 364 runs against Don Bradman's Australians.

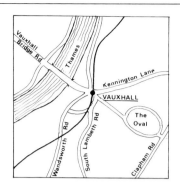

VAUXHALL
Opened 1848
London & South Western
Railway

When the South Western was extended from its original terminus at Nine Elms to Waterloo, most of the new line was built on a viaduct. The only intermediate station was at Vauxhall, named after the fashionable pleasure gardens nearby. It was designed by Sir William Tite, but was burned down in 1856. A second rebuilding took place when the line was widened in 1891, and more recently the station has undergone extensive restoration and modernisation. At one time all incoming trains to Waterloo stopped here for the collection of tickets, which finally ceased in 1916. One of the station's most important functions was as a centre for London's milk traffic; in 1913 four special trains brought in one thousand and five hundred churns a day from the West Country. A serious collision at Vauxhall in 1912, caused by a driver misreading signals, resulted in the deaths of a passenger and a railwayman, and several casualties.

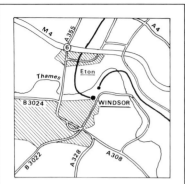

WINDSOR AND ETON

Windsor and Eton Station is more of an experience than a museum. This original Great Western Railway station was built in 1849 by who else but Isambard K. Brunel. Since then it was altered twice before being restored to its original design in 1897 when an extra platform was put in solely for the use of the Royal Family when travelling to Windsor Castle from London Paddington.

Restoration of the station interior includes a small anteroom for the Sovereign's travelling staff, probably only used when Queen Victoria or Edward VII were actually waiting to greet guests arriving for a visit to Windsor. The Royal waiting-room is comfortably and elegantly furnished with exact copies of the original pieces, although the clock on the mantelpiece is original. Attached to the waiting-room is a private retiring-room complete with hand basin and separate toilet. Alongside the platform is a replica of an engine that would have pulled the Royal train, plus two Victorian Diamond Jubilee coaches one of which was found semi-derelict on a caravan park in Wales in 1982. I'll bet the people who used it as sleeping quarters over the years never realised they were snoozing in Royal surroundings.

What makes the whole station museum experience different is the inclusion of an exhibition created by the Madame Tussaud's Company. The exhibition built round the station is quite wonderful. It depicts on the platform side of the station the arrival of the Royal train with the Queen's guests all dressed in the appropriate costumes of 1897. They are waiting to be greeted by Queen Victoria and the Prince and Princess of Wales, later the King and Queen, with all the station and train staff figures going about their duties.

Outside, under the magnificent glass-covered forecourt, the scene changes to a later time when the Queen and her guests can be seen coming out of the station entrance, ready to get into their carriages to travel to nearby Windsor Castle, accompanied by a guard of honour of the Coldstream Guards and the Household Cavalry, many of them in full dress uniforms, plus a military band backing the whole parade. It is a huge pageant of figures re-creating this Royal occasion. Within another part of the building there is a theatre with a continuous unique audio-visual show depicting scenes of some of the personalities of the period (including Queen Victoria) developed by Madame Tussaud's. I should think this is a must on the tourist list when visiting the historic town of Windsor.

By the way, the rest of the station is still used for normal rail travel to and from London Paddington.

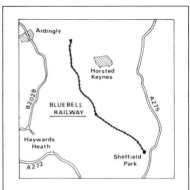

THE BLUEBELL RAILWAY

The Bluebell line between Sheffield Park and Horsted Keynes was once part of a longer cross-country line which ran between Lewes and East Grinstead. This line was promoted in 1876 as the Lewes and East Grinstead Railway Company by a group of local landowners anxious to improve the transportation of goods and products to and from their estates. The Chairman of the company was the Earl of Sheffield whose estate was at Sheffield Park, but even he and the other wealthy backers were unable to meet the full expenses involved in the construction of the line and looked to other existing railway companies for help.

Incidentally the Earl of Sheffield lived in one of the most beautiful houses in Sussex. The magnificent gardens and parkland at Sheffield Park contained his own cricket ground, which was reputed to be one of the finest in the world. The pavilions were quite wonderful and ornate, with marble, gold and blue basins in the washrooms. The Third Earl played host to many Australian touring teams at Sheffield Park and in 1891–2 took an England team to Australia at his own expense. The team, captained by W. G. Grace, proved a great success socially, although Sheffield's side lost by two matches to one. The Earl of Sheffield appreciated the wonderful hospitality of the Australians so much that he presented a gift of £150 to the cricket authorities 'down under' and the money was used to establish the Sheffield Shield, one of the most famous cricket trophies in the world. This magnificent trophy has been played for ever since by the Australian State cricket teams of New South Wales, Victoria, Western Australia, South Australia and more recently Tasmania. In September 1990 an anniversary cricket match between an England XI and an Australian XI was played at the nearby village of Fletching to commemorate the matches played between the two countries at Sheffield Park from 1881–96.

In 1878 the recently formed Lewes and East Grinstead Railway Company, headed by the Earl of Sheffield, approached the London Brighton and South Coast Railway who were at the time most anxious that their rival the South Eastern Railway should not secure a foothold in 'their territory' and thus have access to the lucrative traffic to Brighton and Eastbourne. This gave the London Brighton and South Coast Railway the opportunity to thwart the South Eastern's plans for a railway through Beckenham and Godstone to East Grinstead and thence to Kemp Town, Brighton. So the London Brighton and South Coast Railway agreed to meet debts in land acquisition and construction, and to complete and operate the line.

The Lewes to East Grinstead line was opened on 1st August 1882, and a double-track branch connecting Horsted Keynes Station with the London Brighton and South Coast Railway mainline at Haywards Heath, was opened on 3rd September 1883. Once the line was operational the Lewes and East Grinstead Company passed into oblivion and became part of the London Brighton and South Coast Railway system. The stations themselves were quite lavish, the buildings being in what is often called

the LB&SCR 'country house' design, each one similar but differing in detail.

In the 1930s competition from the motor-bus, coupled with a lack of 'promotion' of the line by the Southern Railway, which had taken over from the LB&SCR in the regional reorganisation of the railways in 1923, caused the passenger traffic, up till then quite healthy, to decline sharply. Upon nationalisation of the railways in 1948 British Railways took over the line and by the early 1950s closure proposals were being made.

Provisions for passengers and freight that had been 'lavish and spacious' when the line was built had now become vastly too expensive to operate and the line closed on 28th May 1955 without ceremony during a rail strike. Then a curious event that was to have far-reaching consequences occurred. Miss Bessemer, a local resident, discovered that the closure was in fact illegal. The original Act of Parliament transferring the operation of the line from the Lewes and East Grinstead Railway Company to the London Brighton and South Coast Railway in 1882 required the latter to run a minimum service of four trains each way per day stopping at specified stations in return for taking over the Lewes and East Grinstead Railway's assets. These commitments were passed to the Southern Railway in 1923 and to British Railways in 1948, so British Railways were compelled to reopen the line and provide the statutory four trains which they did in August 1956. These did not run at very convenient times, the first leaving Lewes at 9.30 a.m. and the last leaving East Grinstead at 4.30 p.m. They did not stop at Barcombe, which was the busiest station on the line, nor at Kingscote, since these were not mentioned in the original Act. Passengers were few, and the consequent heavy losses provided a convincing argument for closure. In the meantime British Railways sought a

THE SHEFFIELD SHIELD

The shield, which measures forty-six by thirty inches, is of silver, flanked with a batsman on one side and a bowler on the other, each solidly modelled with the bat and the ball of gold. On the centre plates is a representation of the Sheffield Park cricket ground, with a full team in their respective places in the field, each man and the pavilion being raised and standing out boldly. The main body of the Shield is of silver, of which two hundred ounces were used; the leaf, shell, and scroll work being in parts oxidised to heighten the general effect. There are sixteen golden inscription plates, to bear the names of successful colonies. The Sheffield and Australian arms resting on the shoulders of the Shield are enamelled in correct colours, and the whole is surmounted by a statue of 'Victory'.

further Act of Parliament to release them from their obligations, and eventually obtained permission to shut down the line. The service was withdrawn on 16th March 1958, by which time the Bluebell line had gained national fame.

It is perhaps not so surprising that a meeting was called in Haywards Heath on 15th March 1959 with the objective of reopening the line. Three students called the meeting which was well-attended and the Lewes and East Grinstead Railway Preservation Society was formed. It was obvious, however, at the initial meeting that to operate the entire line from Lewis to East Grinstead was not a practical proposition. The cost of operating a passenger service over the whole line would be very great and the receipts small. However, it was considered that a section of line could be operated with steam-trains as a tourist attraction using voluntary staff. The Society recommended the section of line from Sheffield Park Station, where there was a good water supply for the locomotives, to a point just south of Horsted Keynes, where there was a connecting line to Haywards Heath, operated by British Rail, to be the most suitable. At the second meeting of the Society this was agreed and the Society's name changed from the Lewes & East Grinstead Railway Preservation Society to the Bluebell Railway Preservation Society.

One of the elected Trustees of the Society was deputed to negotiate with British Railways to purchase or rent this section of line. British Rail had in the meantime intimated that they would be prepared to let the Society rent the booking-office at Sheffield Park at five shillings (25p) per week. It is difficult to imagine how Sheffield Park looked then. It was a rundown country station with a small goods yard consisting of four sidings and a loading dock, all choked with weeds. Restoration work soon commenced, clearing the track, painting the station and overhauling the signalling. Incidentally the footbridge at Sheffield Park is quite unusual. It is double the width of a normal station footbridge and was originally at Lingfield racecourse before being purchased by the railway. The extra width allowed racegoers more freedom of movement when they were in a hurry, which is generally the habit of regular punters.

In 1959 British Railways offered the Society a five-year lease at £2,250

98

per annum and a limited company was set up, The Bluebell Railway Ltd, to take on the legal and financial obligations of operating the railway. The Bluebell Railway opened on 7th August 1960 as the first standard-gauge passenger-carrying preserved railway. From small beginnings Bluebell is now internationally famous and one of the top tourist attractions in Sussex attracting some 300,000 visitors a year.

The Bluebell line, like other preserved railways, has been used for film and television location work. Sheffield Park became Ballater Station for the television series *Edward and Mrs Simpson*. (The original Ballater Station in the Scottish Highlands was used by Royal families when they were visiting Balmoral Castle, and although the line no longer exists the original station building is now a restaurant.)

Late in 1961 the Bluebell Railway was able to operate trains into Horsted Keynes, still a British Rail station, and 1962 and 1963 saw a number of through trains from Victoria to Sheffield Park, via Haywards Heath and Horsted Keynes. On 27th October 1963, however, the line from Haywards Heath closed, cutting off the connecting rail service. This meant that Bluebell was now the sole user of Horsted Keynes.

Bluebell's attention was now turned to raising money for the purchase of the existing line, opening negotiations in 1964. Eventually British Rail and the Bluebell Railway reached agreement in the autumn of 1967 on a purchase price of £43,500 for the line, including a substantial amount of land at Horsted Keynes.

1986 was a landmark for the Bluebell Railway when it became a public company. In the summer of 1984 Kingscote Station, north of Horsted Keynes, came on to the market and despite many years of neglect, was still basically sound. After considerable deliberation an offer was made in excess of £100,000 and this proved sufficient. Kingscote Station is set at the end of an unspoilt and secluded valley and it is difficult to believe that it is less than two miles from the bustling town of East Grinstead.

Planning permission was granted in 1985 to extend the line to rejoin British Rail at East Grinstead. So once again the Bluebell will have a mainline connection with the major rail network.

KENT & EAST SUSSEX RAILWAY

KENT AND EAST SUSSEX RAILWAY

The Kent and East Sussex preserved railway is a descendant of one of the most extraordinary lines in the transport history of this country. The headquarters are at Tenterden, a beautiful example of an English county market town (once a thriving port would you believe) with its wide main street and unusual shops. The Kent and East Sussex Railway was still privately owned when Britain's railways were nationalised in 1948 (it was one of the few that had not been absorbed into one of the big four companies in 1923).

The Kent and East Sussex Railway originally known as the Rother Valley Railway, opened in 1900 and started at Robertsbridge, a junction on the Tonbridge to Hastings line, and ran through initially to Rolvenden near Tenterden. The extension to Tenderden was not completed until 1903, and then later Headcorn on the Tonbridge to Ashford line in 1905, thereby giving this railway access to mainline traffic at either end of the route.

After several years of on/off plans by various companies to link surrounding villages in the south-east Kent and Sussex area with the already established busy lines in the region, a gentleman called Colonel Stephens, a railway engineer, designed and built the Kent and East Sussex Railway. The whole project was not an easy exercise, in some instances the line had to run over the River Rother and also alongside it. The management were well aware of the risk this might bring, endangering schedules and even the lives of passengers and employees. In fact in 1918 flooding did cause a derailment to a parcels' van on Padgham's curve near Bodiam. But Colonel Stephen's talents as an engineer overcame the early difficulties and set-backs, and soon the railway was in use for passenger and freight traffic. Though profits were never large, the local communities were catered for and they remained quite happy with their little railway. By 1926, however, the line had become unprofitable. After the death of Stephens in 1931 the line was kept going for a further sixteen years by his assistant Mr Austen, though nobody quite knows how.

In 1923 Stephens had experimented with a new form of rail transport – two Ford road buses linked back to back and fitted with metal wheels in place of normal road wheels. This experiment was so successful that the buses remained in use until the Second World War. The ride was pretty rough, earning the buses the nickname of 'The Bumper'. Although many improvements to the line were made by British Rail in 1948 the line did not last long after this and was closed to passengers in January 1954, and the track from Tenterden to Headcorn was removed. The remaining section remained open for goods traffic, but that too succumbed to the inevitable in 1961. The railway had become a local institution and a society was formed with the object of preserving the line from Tenterden to Robertsbridge, but there was a thirteen-year struggle ahead of them, very much in keeping with the original struggles that had occurred before the line was first built at the turn of the century. After much heart-searching and years of exhaustive legal battles, it was decided that

Opposite: Ellen Terry country at Tenterden

the future of preservation lay in the section between Tenterden town and Bodiam only. The Tenterden Railway Company was formed in 1973 and the rebuilding of bridges and stations and replacement of sleepers began, assisted by the Royal Engineers and the Kent County Council. Progress was initially made as far as Wittersham, and the station was reopened by the Rt Hon Edward Heath in 1978. Although Bodiam has not quite yet been reached it will be in the not-too-distant future. When it is, it will bring many benefits to the Kent and East Sussex Railway because of course Bodiam and its castle is very high on the list of tourist attractions.

This little railway has also played host to royalty. On 9th June 1982 Her Majesty Queen Elizabeth the Queen Mother visited Tenterden as the Lord Warden of the Cinque Ports, and as part of her duties that day she was asked to inaugurate a specially adapted coach for disabled people. The coach was named 'Petros' after Peter Sinclair, a sufferer from muscular dystrophy, whose father David was the instigator of the project. The conversion work was carried out by apprentices of British Rail's Southern Region CM&EE and the materials paid for by many fund-raising activities and donations from local firms. The Queen Mother travelled the two miles to Rolvenden on the special train and spoke to most of the disabled people in the coach, which was the first to operate on any preserved railway – or any other railway for that matter.

The Duke of Gloucester was in Northiam on 4th June 1990. A helicopter of the Royal Flight landed in a field adjacent to Northiam Station. The Duke alighted and walked the short distance to the station entrance. This visit was the culmination of many months of detailed planning and hard work by the volunteer workforce of the railway. Over one hundred guests were conveyed from Tenterden for the occasion, and after being introduced by the chairman, David Stratton, to the members who had made an outstanding contribution to the extension, the Duke unveiled a plaque commemorating his visit. He then joined driver Colin Edwards on the footplate of the engine 'Sutton' and drove the train down the platform, breaking a white tape stretched over the line. Northiam was officially opened.

One of this country's most talented and loveliest actresses, Ellen Terry (later Dame Ellen) was a regular traveller on the railway when she lived at nearby Smallhythe. When she was relaxing in the country during her busy life in the theatre she was often seen riding around the local lanes in her own pony and trap. Her lovely house was built in the first half of the sixteenth century, soon after practically the whole village was destroyed by fire. Smallhythe is only a couple of miles from Tenterden and the whole of this area is a beautiful part of the country. If you are in the vicinity of Tenterden, and once you have visited the town station of course, try and spare an hour to visit Ellen's house. It is now owned by the National Trust who were bequeathed it by her daughter Edith Craig. It is more than a memorial to the great actress, it is a treasure-trove of theatrical memorabilia concerning not only her long association with Henry Irving but also so many other famous theatrical names such as Beerbohm Tree, Madge Kendall, Sarah Siddons, Edmund and Charles Kean, George Alexander, and many more. Ellen was a great collector of mementos and the house still contains much of these.

Colonel Stephens' railway is once again giving much pleasure to its travellers, so it just goes to show what determination and hard work can achieve just as it did in the building of the original railway. As it says on a notice-board at the station:

THE PAST – The Railway was opened in 1900 and is of historical interest in being the first to be built under the 1896 Light Railways Act. It was one of the 16 lines engineered or managed by the late Lt. Col. Holman F. Stephens. It remained independent until 1948 when it was nationalised. The line originally ran 21 miles from Robertsbridge to Headcorn. Following closure to passengers in 1954 the railway lay semi-derelict until re-opened in 1974 by the Tenterden Railway Company.

THE FUTURE – The railway is now the last example of the once numerous standard gauge independent passenger-carrying light railways. The Tenterden Railway Company which now operates the line is a voluntary organisation and is registered as an educational charity. 10 miles of the original railway has been saved and train services will be extended towards Bodiam in stages as funds permit. To fulfil its aims the railway depends upon visitors riding on its trains. Thank you for your support!

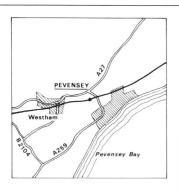

PEVENSEY & WESTHAM
Opened 1846
London Brighton & South Coast Railway

Many stations have had a change in name, not a few reverting to the original one, like Pevensey. It started life as Westham & Pevensey and then for ten months in 1851 became Pevensey & Westham, before settling down as plain Pevensey until Westham was added again in 1890. Since that time the railway authorities seem to have been fairly sure just where the station is, even though the name is still misleading as the station is actually in Westham, three quarters of a mile from Pevensey which, just to add to the confusion, has its own Pevensey Bay halt.

The main station building is not the original, having been rebuilt, probably in the 1870s, in the unpretentious manner one would expect at a small country station of that period.

PEVENSEY

I've driven many times down what local people in the area call the Pevensey straight. This is a long road that runs from a spot near Pevensey Castle in Sussex to Cooden near Bexhill-on-Sea. Either side of this long road the area is completely flat, and was all part of the sea port of Pevensey before it was reclaimed from the English Channel. The Romans built the fort of Anderida on a spit of land then open to the sea. It fell to the Saxons in AD 491.

When William the Conqueror landed in Pevensey Bay in 1066 he had a castle built on the site of the then-ruined fort. Large remains of the castle still exist and you can also see, if you look hard, part of the pill-boxes that were built into the ancient walls of the remains in the Second World War. These pill-boxes would have been armed and used to cover the low-lying land already mentioned. A Government Mint was built in Pevensey village in the fourteenth century. In the sixteenth century Henry VIII's physician, Dr Andrew Borde, bought it and altered it as his residence. The building is still standing as The Old Mint House.

RAMSGATE

The harbour of this Thanet seaside town was built in the eighteenth century and over the years has become a thriving and busy port. In Victorian times it developed as a fashionable resort much-liked by Londoners. Sickly children were sent there to improve their health and benefit from the fine sea air. Today there is a large yacht marina.

For many years Ramsgate was the home of actor John le Mesurier, after he decided that the noise and fumes of London were not conducive to relaxation. John had abandoned driving a car in the 1970s 'because people keep tooting me up', and he became a regular rail traveller to and from Ramsgate Station. He always remarked on the politeness of the staff, and certainly I know that one of them, John O'Connor, is also a keen gardener and makes sure the station has plenty of flowers around the place.

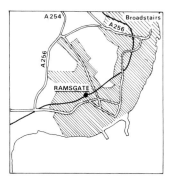

RAMSGATE
Opened 1926
Southern Railway

The Southern Railway's architect, J. R. Scott, designed the new station for Ramsgate, which replaced two terminal stations, Ramsgate Town of the South Eastern Railway and Ramsgate Harbour of the fiercely competing London Chatham & Dover. The station was built on a new connecting line that enabled through-trains to run between Chatham and Ashford via the Thanet coast. Along with neighbouring Margate, the building is typical of its period, its lofty, spacious booking-hall providing ample capacity for large numbers of commuters and day-trippers alike.

Summer days at Ramsgate

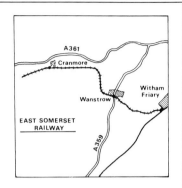

EAST SOMERSET RAILWAY
'THE STRAWBERRY LINE'

'The man who loves giants' has become synonymous over the years with that fine artist David Shepherd. Although the 'giants' are associated mainly with his beautiful paintings of African elephants and other wild-life creatures, you may not be aware of his other giants, two wonderful steam-engines which run on his preserved East Somerset Railway. David bought these two locomotives, *Black Prince* and *Green Knight* in 1967 out of the proceeds of an exhibition of his paintings in New York. Once he had purchased them he had to find a permanent home for them, but that didn't materialise until much later, but materialise he was sure it would. If you knew the man you would not be surprised at his succeeding in anything he set his sights on, although I'm sure he would tell you that not all of his proposed projects have borne fruit at the first attempt, and anyway those that have succeeded have entailed blood, sweat and not a few tears.

First of all let's go back in time to the heady days of railway development in the south-west, and particularly in the Somerset area.

Unless you look at a railway map of the 1850s you cannot conceive just how many different railway companies were operating in this comparatively small area of the country. Bordered by Frome in the east, Weston-super-Mare in the west, Bath to the north, and Taunton in the south, there was the Wilts, Somerset and Weymouth, the Midland, the Bristol and Exeter, the Somerset and Dorset, the Bristol and North Somerset and the Great Western. Into this web of railways came the East Somerset. Isambard Kingdom Brunel had a hand in its conception (wouldn't you know) but then he was the genius behind the establishment of the Great Western which was spreading its wings all over the west of England, actually at that time using the broad-gauge system.

Once the East Somerset was opened from Witham, just south of Frome, to Shepton Mallet on 9th November 1858, there were rumblings from the nearby city of Wells. They felt that they deserved to be part of the extension to give them a link with London. They did have some rail communication with a station on the Somerset Central Railway but Wells wanted more than that, and one would have thought quite rightly so. It was, and still is, an ecclesiastical centre with its magnificent cathedral and historical buildings that make it a natural target for tourists. Times have not changed as far as this is concerned.

The East Somerset Railway extension from Shepton Mallet to Wells was eventually opened on 28th February 1862 and the city had got its wish. The arrival in Wells of the first train was celebrated by the Mayor and Corporation, in scarlet ceremonial robes, the Bishop of Bath and Wells and a band playing the National Anthem, followed by a luncheon for fifty of the principal participants at the Swan Hotel.

In 1874 the Great Western Railway decided to change from broad gauge to the now conventional standard system and suggested that the

East Somerset Railway should do the same, but they did not have the finance to do this, and were promptly absorbed into the Great Western Railway. It was certainly no good having a small railway company with one gauge and the more powerful and established one with another.

The Great Western Railway had the resources and access to all the labour they needed so the change-over took place during the weekend of 19th to 21st June 1874; a great feat of reconstruction in such a short space of time. The plate layers engaged on the conversion came mainly from the Oxford area and were brought in by special train. They were allowed to drink any amount of oatmeal and water, sweetened by sugar, which was found to quench the thirst better than beer or cider and give the men stamina. (It sounds revolting to me.) Each workman was expected to bring his own shovel, rug and greatcoat, also a coffee or tea can, and had to sign a declaration that they would not leave the site (except for certain purposes!) from dawn until dusk. They were provided with sheds to sleep in with straw on the floor and received an average of 3 shillings (15 pence) per day plus a generous ration allowance of 1s/3d (approx 6p).

The first experimental journey to run a train on the new gauge took place late on the Sunday of the weekend in question, without passengers. The train had good-looking carriages mounted on six wheels and fitted with patent buffers to steady the train and 'prevent concussion'. The 2nd-class seats were padded with back and head rests, and 1st-class passengers had handsome domed coaches with gilt mouldings. So there it was, the East Somerset Railway in the space of forty-eight hours was now under the management of the Great Western Railway, and the original name was not to be used again for nearly a hundred years when that man of many parts, David Shepherd, reopened a part of it, and once again brought the sound of steam back to this small area of Somerset.

How did this all come about? Well as I've said, David, having bought his two engines, needed a line to run them on. He tried desperately to save the Longmoor Military Railway in Hampshire where his engines were then housed. This failed, so he and his friends scoured the country

107

for a new site. Until a new home was found a rent of £20 a week had to be paid to British Rail for the use of a siding near Southampton. Finally he was told of a derelict portion of line and a station at Cranmore in Somerset, part of the original East Somerset Railway. The great advantage about this line was that it was still connected to British Rail mainline which meant the two engines and any future rolling-stock could be moved to Cranmore without too much difficulty. If you look out of the window between Frome and Castle Cary you will see the sign, East Somerset Junction (Witham).

It would be impossible in this small space to describe everything that David Shepherd and his wife Avril and their family have achieved since taking over the Cranmore Railway (now once again the East Somerset). After clearing the line, restoring the derelict station, and building a fine, Victorian-style engine-shed on the site of the old one, they began to tackle other refinements, including the refurbishment of a wonderful gents' loo, that David suggests was used by Isambard Kingdom . . . (well you know who I mean!). A new ladies' loo had to be built, and a restaurant and shop are in the process of construction.

The signal-box is now a gallery for David's paintings and sketches of wildlife and railway subjects, although a larger building for this purpose may be erected somewhere on the site later.

The railway now goes as far as Mendip Vale, just short of Shepton Mallet, and a station building will be put up on the platform there, which incidentally was built by the present company.

Naturally David's love of wildlife is not neglected. There is a small sanctuary near Cranmore and plenty of animal life to see on the trip to Mendip Vale; badgers, foxes, deer etc. Just how near David must have been to bankruptcy during the setting up of his dream we'll never know.

Royalty and film stars alike have come to visit this little railway that has tried, and is still trying, to think of everything to please its customers. There is a carpark for visitors, with a children's play area and picnic space. You are asked to try to keep it as clean as possible because as David says, 'If the platforms, public areas and particularly the toilets, are kept generally clean and wholesome then the public will follow suit and keep it that way.' I should like to add that I've always believed in this philosophy for our theatres in this country. If we want people to be conscious of cleanliness when visiting public buildings it is first impressions that count.

The whole railway project is run under a charitable status with the title of The East Somerset Railway Company Limited. In increasingly difficult times with ever-escalating costs involved in running a preserved line, the East Somerset Railway nevertheless looks forward to a secure future. A major development for example in 1990 has been the long-awaited arrival at Cranmore of the British-built locomotive that had worked in Africa for seventy-eight years and which, together with a magnificent 1927-built railway coach, was given to David by President Kaunda of Zambia.

As David says, 'With the help of the visiting public, the devoted volunteer-staff and small experienced paid workforce, we will achieve our aims, so please tell your friends to come and see us.' The whole concept of the preservation of this little railway is a great credit in the first instance to the Shepherd family, and long may it prosper.

ISAMBARD KINGDOM BRUNEL

by Alex Metcalf

The development and practical application of the steam-engine was to change the lives of not only the British but people all over the world.

Many men had experimented with steam, notably Newcomen in 1705 (not very successfully), and James Watt, who in 1769 patented the first high-pressure engine. However, it was not until 1804 when the Cornish engineer, Richard Trevithick, built a locomotive that actually ran (at 5 mph!), from Merthyr Tydfil to a nearby canal in South Wales, that the birth of the 'Iron Horse' really began.

In 1815 came Stephenson's *Rocket* and ten years later he built the Stockton to Darlington railway, the world's first passenger line. In 1769, the same year that Watt patented his steam-engine, a French engineer named Marc Brunel was born. He was twenty-four years old when he was forced to flee from the French 'Reign of Terror' and went to America, where he continued his civil-engineering career. Six years later he settled in England, and was responsible for a number of mechanical inventions, including a knitting machine. He designed and built, with his son, the Thames Tunnel from Wapping to Rotherhithe completed in 1843, and earned himself a Knighthood.

Marc Brunel was a great lover of England and a royalist, and when his son was born in 1806 he named him Isambard Kingdom Brunel, in honour of his adopted country. I. K. Brunel was to become the greatest civil engineer and shipbuilder in our history. Isambard was appointed to build the Great Western Railway from London to Bristol, and then further down to the West country. His work was so well-designed and executed that today it is still one of the fastest stretches of BR, enabling great speeds to be achieved between our cities. This incredibly talented man designed and built railways, stations, bridges, tunnels, and even atmospheric pumping stations, one of which is at Starcross, near Exeter.

He also turned his talents to shipbuilding, the first of his ships being built for the Great Western Railway. She was named the *Great Western*, a paddle-steamer launched in 1838, and was the first ship specially built for the transatlantic trade, making the crossing in a little over fifteen days. She was of 1320 tons and carried 240 passengers. Five years later he built the *Great Britain*, the first ship to have an iron hull and propeller drive. She was of 3,270 tons, had six masts, and carried 360 passengers and up to 1,200 tons of cargo. This famous ship was eventually found derelict in the Falkland Islands, and was salvaged and restored.

Finally in 1858 he laid down the keel for what was the greatest ship of that time, the *Great Eastern*. This giant vessel (originally to be named *Leviathan*) was of nearly 19,000 tons, 692 feet long, and was driven by both paddles and propeller. She had five funnels, six masts, and could carry 4,000 passengers and 400 crew. Brunel had intended her to do the India–Australia run, but plagued by many technical difficulties and by then severely short of cash he died at the early age of fifty-three before the ship was launched. So ended the career of England's greatest railway pioneer and shipbuilder.

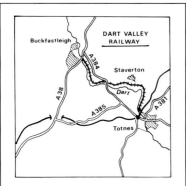

THE DART VALLEY AND PAIGNTON AND DARTMOUTH RAILWAYS

In the early reign of Queen Victoria one area of the country that was under discussion for further railway expansion was South Devon. A number of routes were under consideration, including one from Exeter along the coast through Torquay and the Dart estuary area crossing the South Hams to reach Plymouth, but in due course the route via Teignmouth, Newton Abbot and Totnes was chosen. Brunel was so sure that the former would be the eventual route with a bridge over the Dart estuary from Kingswear to Dartmouth, that a station was built there on the quay. So that lovely Devon resort had a railway station without a railway and Dartmouth Station is recorded in the Guinness Book of Railway Records as being the only station in Britain to have never had a train. In later years the ferry connecting Kingswear to Dartmouth was managed by the Great Western Railway and it was possible to book your ticket at Dartmouth Station. The station is still on the quay, but it is now a restaurant, so you can have a reasonably priced meal or snack overlooking this beautiful spot. To get back to the eventual route that was decided upon. It put Torquay, Paignton and Kingswear on a branch line from Newton Abbot.

We'll now turn to the other branch that was to eventually concern the Dart Valley Railway Company before their involvement in the Paignton to Kingswear line. This was the Totnes to Ashburton line via Staverton and Buckfastleigh. It was apparent very early on in the forming of the Dart Valley Railway Company that Ashburton would have to be excluded from their plans, as the Ministry of Transport had indicated that they were to build a major road, the A38, across the Buckfastleigh to Ashburton stretch of the line so Buckfastleigh was immediately thought of as the home base of the Dart Valley Railway. Incidentally the front of Ashburton Station is still in existence and is used as a garage and coach station. So next time you travel from Exeter to Plymouth on the A38 remember you're driving over what was the Buckfastleigh to Ashburton section of the line.

We shall describe the journey from the Buckfastleigh end. It is difficult to suggest on which side of the train you should sit, for the views are equally glorious on both sides, but for much of the way the river itself is on the right of the train leaving Buckfastleigh. The train gently gathers speed and soon after leaving the station you can glimpse on the left the large butterfly house and the otter sanctuary at the edge of the carpark just before the train crosses the River Mardle, one of the tributary streams of the Dart. The banks and cuttings of the railway are the home of many wild flowers and the Dart is an important river for angling. Watch out too for the various birds here, especially the species that comes high on my list, the kingfisher. Those brightly coloured little chaps diving and swooping over the water are glorious.

A passing loop heralds the approach of Staverton Bridge Station. The station has a single platform and the small signal-box here is of interest

Left: Approaching Kingswear on the Dartmouth Railway

Below: Staverton Station

since it was in use as a garden shed in the grounds of the local rectory. It was repossessed in exchange for building a new shed for the rector! Staverton Station will be a familiar sight to many, for it has been used on several occasions to provide an old-time country station setting for films and television serials, particularly *To Serve Them All My Days*, *A Horseman Riding By*, and *The Hound of the Baskervilles*.

The level-crossing beyond Staverton Mill is always known as Knapper's Crossing after Mrs Knapper, a well-loved local character who operated the crossing gates for many years. In more recent years another venerable lady, Florrie Whitefoot, looked after the crossing and only had to give up the job, well into her eighties, because of ill health.

It was a very Gilbertian situation when the Dart Valley Railway was officially opened by the late Lord Beeching (formerly Dr Richard Beeching) on 21st May 1969. The Doctor of course had been prominent in the closure. During the 1970s the Dart Valley Railway built their own station called Totnes Riverside alongside the junction with British Rail on the east bank of the River Dart, but unfortunately with no facility for passengers to join or leave trains there.

If you've enjoyed the Dart Valley journey I'm sure you'll want to travel on the Paignton and Dartmouth Steam Railway. When it was realised that British Railways intended to withdraw passenger services between Paignton and Kingswear the Dart Valley management immediately started negotiations and at the same time changed the structure of the company into a public company, the Dart Valley Light Railway PLC. That line is now known as the Paignton and Dartmouth Steam Railway.

You may be curious why having saved one line the Dart Valley Light Railway PLC should operate a second line in the same area. In fact the two lines are totally dissimilar in character. The original Dart Valley line from Buckfastleigh is, as I have said, purely a branch line, while the Paignton to Kingswear line, although of single track, was in fact fully up to mainline standards and able to carry the largest and heaviest locomotives ever to run on British Railways. In fact in 1973 the world-famous LNER engine *Flying Scotsman* worked on the Paignton and Dartmouth Steam Railway. The line is situated right in the heart of the important Torbay holiday area, starting in the midst of Paignton town centre adjoining the British Rail station. This building was put up by the Paignton and Dartmouth Steam Railway (Dart Valley PLC) and it boasts a shop, snack bar and the George Jackson Churchward Lecture Theatre. George Jackson Churchward was one of the foremost and famous railway engineers of his time. He was Chief Mechanical Engineer of the Great Western Railway, the son of a Paignton farmer and born in Stoke Gabriel, a fact of which the Paignton and Dartmouth Steam Railway are justly proud. The Lecture Theatre itself is a replica of the type of News Theatre found on many stations in the 1930s. It is fully equipped to show films from 8mm to 35mm, wide screen and video.

Adjacent to the station forecourt is perhaps the most unusual feature of the company, the Torbay Cinema. It is owned by the Paignton and Dartmouth Steam Railway and is the oldest remaining purpose-built cinema in Western Europe. Originally called The Paignton Picture House it was opened in the early 1900s and has a beautiful barrel ceiling in the auditorium. In the ceiling décor there are some unusual facial carvings depicting famous film stars, such as Mary Pickford and Douglas Fairbanks. In the cinema's heyday, when it had stage presentations as well, it also had a twenty-one piece orchestra, and private boxes in the balcony. This pretty little cinema still has regular film shows and is managed by John Mann, a member of the Torbay Railway Society.

During the original construction of this line in the 1850s a celebration was laid on when the first section of the line to Paignton was completed in 1859, with the cooking and distribution of a huge Paignton Pudding and all the 'navvies' who had worked on the line, together with their families, were entertained by the company. The pudding, made of 1,900 pounds of meat and bread, was washed down with cider and conveyed in procession on a wagon drawn by eight horses. After the pudding arrived on Paignton Green the invited guests sat down inside the rope barrier while the rest of Paignton gathered round outside. The pudding was now ready for distribution, and that's when the trouble started! The barrier was broken down, with the people outside clamouring for a piece of the pudding. The invited guests, the five policemen, the committee and the people of Paignton became one seething mass on the ground. There were 18,000 people on the ground that day, and by the time order was restored not a morsel of the Paignton Pudding remained!

For the first three-quarters of a mile the line runs parallel with that of its larger neighbour British Railways, whose mainline trains arriving at Paignton sometimes continue forward over the other single track to reach Goodrington carriage sidings, used particularly on summer Saturdays for stabling and preparation of stock on holiday trains. By the time we reach Goodrington platform we can see the sea, but at the same time it signifies the start of the very stiff two-and-a-half-mile climb to Churston.

The train then crosses two viaducts before veering away inland to Churston Station. This station's claim to fame is that it was regularly used by the thriller writer Agatha Christie who lived nearby. She would travel to London from here to see her literary agent, via Newton Abbot, arriving with the manuscript of her latest novel. It was on one of the return journeys that Agatha Christie got the idea for one of her best-known thrillers, *The 4.20 from Paddington.*

Just before Churston is the turntable. Because of curves on the line the wheels on one side tend to wear more than those on the other, so now and again, between seasons, the engines and coaches are turned as required to even out the wear. Churston was the junction for the branch line to Brixham and was originally called Brixham Road, then renamed Churston when the Brixham branch was built. This short line was built to handle the fish traffic from the small port of Brixham. The branch itself was built by a man who was driver, fireman, station-master and general factotum. He drove himself into bankruptcy (and mad I should think!) and the branch was 'bailed out' by the South Devon Railway which was itself eventually absorbed by the Great Western Railway. Brixham was also the home of the famous red sail trawlers, which were the subject of the song 'Red Sails in the Sunset' sung by those two well-known personalities Suzette Tari and Bing Crosby. It was also the landing place of William of Orange when he came to claim the Crown of England.

FATE

An incident that occurred during the height of the Blitz on Plymouth really makes you wonder if occasionally there isn't some unseen guiding influence controlling a situation. In March 1941 George Worth, the relief signalman at the St Budeaux West signal-box just outside the city, saw a large incendiary bomb drop on the line. Knowing a train might be due, even though fires were raging everywhere, and the possibility of it being a munitions' train which were frequently running on the line at that time, he jumped down from the signal-box, and clutching a sandbag ran along the line to try to smother the bomb before it took hold. When he reached the incendiary he heard the loud whistle of a high-explosive bomb coming down, and immediately threw himself to the ground. There was a huge explosion and his pocket watch was smashed although he was uninjured. As he looked back along the line the smoke was clearing, but his signal-box had received a direct hit and was no more.

George owed his life to a German fire-bomb. Makes you think!

My father, Jim Harris, was one of the signalmen at the Devon end of Royal Albert Bridge, Saltash, during the Second World War. One night, when raids were frequent, a passenger-train coming up from Cornwall called at Saltash Station. A lady passenger on the train asked a porter if it was Keyham Station, and he replied, 'No, next stop Madam.' It must be remembered that this was during the black-out, no lights were displayed at stations or elsewhere. The train left and crossed the bridge from Cornwall into Plymouth, Devon. On its way over, my father received a call to warn all trains of imminent air attack (a 'red' warning). He had to stop the train and warn the driver and as he did so, a horrific scream was heard. In the darkness the lady passenger had opened the carriage door and stepped out, there was no platform and she broke a leg. She was assisted by service personnel in the train who used the long seat cushions as a stretcher, and the train then proceeded to the nearest station where an ambulance was waiting. All this when enemy aircraft were approaching, sirens sounding, searchlights weaving and waving, and guns firing!!

Walter Harris

When the Paignton and Dartmouth Steam Railway took over the line there was just a single track through Churston so only one train could be run at a time on the whole route. Within a few years it was clear a more frequent service would be needed to cope with holiday crowds – indeed in the late 1970s the mid-afternoon train from Kingswear was often loaded to ten coaches, with many passengers standing almost in London rush-hour conditions, certainly not anyone's idea of a holiday trip.

From Churston to Kingswear the line starts to go downhill in rolling countryside with wooded slopes bordering the Dart estuary. As the train runs along the water's edge a gradually expanding vista of Dartmouth Harbour is opened up with its mass of yachts and other small craft, with the occasional larger vessel including sailing ships for this is *Onedin Line* country where many of the location shots were filmed for this famous television series. Across the water on the hillside can be seen the Britannia Royal Naval College. The train continues for a further three-quarters of a mile, eases round the righthand curve and approaches Kingswear platform, still at the water's edge.

I have a special affection for Kingswear Station as it was (almost) the end of a journey from London that gave us our first holiday after the last war. I shall always remember the excitement of that particular holiday. Coming from London in a very long train pulled by a very big engine and being in wonderment of the sea almost brushing the carriages through Dawlish Warren, a sea bright blue against the background of the dark-red sand, excitement growing all the time as our ultimate destination, a small and very comfortable guest-house up a hill in Dartmouth, grew nearer. Kingswear looks today just as it did then.

Now for the last stage, on the ferry across the Dart estuary to Dartmouth. There is enough in Dartmouth itself to occupy you for the whole day, but you may like to take a boat trip up the River Dart to Dittesham and back. I did this trip in the early seventies with my very young son and my wife, in the company of Walter Landauer, of Rawicz and Landauer fame, and the great bird and animal impressionist Percy Edwards. My son has never forgotten Percy telling us about all the wildlife which inhabited the banks of the Dart and the river itself, and in the process giving us a detailed impression of all the sounds created by these creatures.

The Station Restaurant at Dartmouth

LOOE

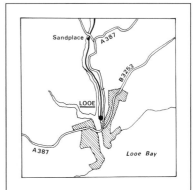

This bathing resort and yachting centre on the south coast of Cornwall, which also offers offshore shark fishing and sea trips, gained its popularity like most other fishing villages from the coming of the railways. The fact that it had a station at all was due to the mining of copper ore and granite around Caradon on the edge of Bodmin Moor. Originally a short standard-gauge railway had been in operation from Caradon where the loaded trucks descended by gravity down the steep gradient to Moorswater near Liskeard. The empties were then drawn back up by horses. From Moorswater the ore and stone went by canal to Looe.

Because the canal was unable to cope with the traffic, the Liskeard and Looe Canal Company decided to build an extension of the railway along the canal bank to Looe Harbour where the cargo was loaded on to boats.

The first train from Moorswater to Looe ran in December 1860, but the two little railways remained nominally independent, although the Caradon line operated the Looe line until 1901 by which time it was bankrupt and the arrangement was reversed. Mining continued to thrive at Caradon until the mid 1870s when a sudden decline set in and thousands were put out of work. Many subsequently left this country to find employment in the Americas. As far as granite was concerned cheaper supplies were discovered in Aberdeen, Norway and Sweden.

Looe in the meantime was beginning to thrive as a tourist centre, so the closing of the mine didn't worry the resort too much. In 1901 the railway was connected to the Great Western mainline at Liskeard, and the passenger services from there on the mainline from London and elsewhere became busier and busier. In 1909 the Great Western Railway took over the running of the branch line, and then of course in 1948 British Rail.

The present station at Looe is not in the same place as the original one. It is farther away from the harbour, and is now a very small building with a sort of bus shelter on the platform. When you change at Liskeard for Looe you wonder which platform to use. In fact you have to actually go out of the station and across a narrow road and there is the second Liskeard Station (for Looe) at right angles to the main line.

It is a peculiar journey to Looe, at least to start with. The train, which comprises diesel rail buses, curves sharply to the right out of the station, under the main line, and drops steeply down to Coombe Junction, where you are now some one hundred and fifty feet below where you first started. The train then reverses and sets off for Looe via St Keyne, Causeland and Sandplace. Looe itself is unmanned, and has a single line, but that is not to say it is neglected. The local Women's Institute looks after it, and this little station has its quota of flowers and shrubs for people to enjoy.

When I was standing on the platform with the view of the sea in the background, and the sun glimmering through the trees from the direction of Liskeard and falling on to the flowers, I thought this is another station where we have to give our thanks to the WI.

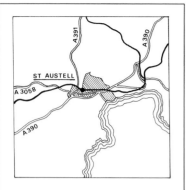

ST AUSTELL

St Austell is on the main London to Penzance line in Cornwall, and as you come upon the station from the approach road there is little hint of what lies behind the late Victorian station buildings. It is a typical Great Western Railway station (GWR were the original owners) and the most striking legacy is the ornate footbridge. Like the rest of the station it is painted in green and a dull red, and the company initials are embossed on the ironwork, circled and picked out in gold. The supports to the platform seats have been given the same treatment, and the letters GWR are entwined in the iron supports.

However, the most pleasing sights are the flower-beds crammed with every conceivable variety of plant, and standing proud and healthy above it all three beautiful palm trees, giving a sub-tropical air to the scene. The flowers are grown at the station in a small cabin which doubles as a greenhouse, and are planted out and looked after by porters David Borlase and Barry Oliver. They obviously love flowers and are a credit to British Rail. I do hope David and Barry receive the recognition they deserve from British Rail and the passengers who use the station.

I also hope that some madman in London (all decisions are made there) doesn't get it into his head to have this station unmanned, and in so doing allow this lovely example of the Great Western Railway to fall into decay. I promise I will go down there myself quite happily and demonstrate with the whole of St Austell if this were to come about!

ST ERTH

St Erth is a station that has been well cared for by its staff. Flower baskets, tubs and platforms are bright with blooms and shrubs carefully nurtured by Cyril Howes and John Cocker, two of the resident British Rail personnel at the station. This, combined with the clean platforms, make waiting for a train a pleasure and you'll find the staff ready to talk about their plants and the history of the station, which is a listed building and most attractive, although it could do with a lick of paint (British Rail take note). There is a rumour that the station may become unmanned at some future date, even though it is on the main Penzance line from London. If this were to happen, and if by any chance it was de-listed, this very pleasant junction could be the victim of developers and of course all the lovely plants and flowers which are now in evidence would be a thing of the past. The station must be looked after by British Rail and not allowed to become a modern architect's toy because of somebody's stupid whim. I have the feeling that the stubborn Cornish people of St Erth would have plenty to say if unmanning became more than a rumour.

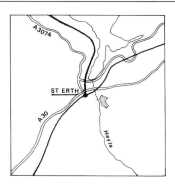

ST ERTH
Opened in 1852
West Cornwall Railway

The original station on this site was named St Ives Road, but when it became a junction on the opening of the St Ives' branch in 1877 the name was changed to St Erth. The St Ives' branch was the last one to be built to Brunel's seven-foot broad gauge. From 1874–6 the station was rebuilt in readiness for its new function as a junction, with a neat stone building with round-headed windows but still only a single mainline platform and the addition of a bay for the branch trains. In the latter year the West Cornwall was taken over by the Great Western, and in 1899 the line was doubled from Hayle to St Erth, when the down (Penzance) platform was probably added, and a small stone waiting-room built on it in the current GWR style.

The St Ives' bay platform is unusual in being at a lower level than the adjoining mainline platform, requiring a curious sloping top to the awning. Apart from additional awnings at the east end of the two mainline platforms, and the removal of the one on the small down side building, the station retains most of its earlier character.

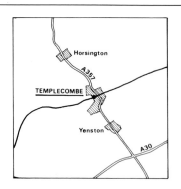

TEMPLECOMBE
Opened 1860
London & South Western
Railway

Opened as a junction where the London & South Western mainline crossed the Somerset & Dorset line, Templecombe rapidly became an important traffic centre with extensive sidings and an engine-shed. As a result, the small village developed into a railway community. A peculiarity of operations was that all trains on the Somerset & Dorset line between Bath and Bournemouth had to reverse up or down a steep, sharp curve into the station, involving two changes of direction. All this changed when the Somerset & Dorset line was closed in 1966. Templecombe was no longer a junction and the station, which the Southern Railway had rebuilt in brick and concrete in the late 1930s, was closed at the same time. Some years later a group of local people began agitating for the station to be reopened, eventually with success.

TEMPLECOMBE

Reopened in 1983 after seventeen years as a ghost station, Templecombe is something of a modern railway miracle. Once a very busy junction for the Southern Railway's London to Exeter route and the much-loved but now extinct Somerset and Dorset Railway, Templecombe is now quite a small station in comparison with the old days.

It was really the local community who were responsible for the reopening of this station. Templecombe and the surrounding area was expanding quickly so suggestions were put by various local societies and business managements to the Somerset County Council and to British Railways with a view to bringing their station into use again.

All parties concerned were in favour of reopening the station and the rebuilding of it became a Templecombe community project, organised by a special working committee. The signal-box was still in place and just had to be brought slightly up-to-date, but the lower half of it has been transformed into a smart waiting-room. There are flowering tubs, hanging baskets and flower-beds on show, including a huge 'Templecombe' beautifully designed in one bed with many varieties of flowers. It is most impressive when you see this as the train draws into the station. The staff and members of various local societies make sure the flowers are always cared for.

The line has been made single here, which is a fairly curious sight on such a busy line but it doesn't cause any problems. British Rail put money into the project and wanted to be assured of some return but they were sceptical as to whether the scheme would really be financially worthwhile. To their surprise, and I suspect to some local people as well, expectations were surpassed. Templecombe was again taking money but more important still, proving that a station was needed. It is also well used by tourists in the area. By the way Templecombe is derived from the Knights Templars, the same bunch of lads that London's Temple Bar was named after.

Templecombe is a wonderful starting point to explore the surrounding countryside. For those of you interested in the Arthurian legends, Cadbury Camp is not far away. A magnificent prehistoric earthwork, reputed to be the site of King Arthur's Camelot. A few miles away to the west is the Roman town of Ilchester, situated on the old Fosse Way and in the town hall there can be seen a thirteenth-century mace, believed to be the oldest staff of office in England, and possibly in Europe. Also within striking distance is the beautiful National Trust Elizabethan House of Montacute, surrounded by the celebrated gardens.

After all this sightseeing, nothing quenches the thirst better than a flagon of Somerset cider, and in the village of Dowlish Wake just to the south-west of Montacute there is a fine collection of old cider-making equipment – jars, bottles and firkins (small barrels) and ancient farm machinery.

SOMERSET & DORSET RAILWAY.
COMPANY RULE

Enginemen are Forbidden to blow their Whistles or Drain Cocks whilst standing in the station, as this may frighten horses and alarm passengers. Furthermore, Leaking Cocks must be attended to. A fine of Sixpence for each Leaking Cock will be strictly enforced.

1864   By Order

WEST SOMERSET RAILWAY

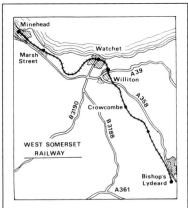

FLAG CONFUSION ON THE WEST SOMERSET RAILWAY AT CROWCOMBE
a true story

Way back, when our station was a 'request' stop, it was customary for the guard to show the driver a red or green flag just before the train reached the platform – to indicate to the driver whether or not there were passengers to get off. However, one day when I was on duty, waiting at the station with no passengers to get on, a train came to a stop with a rather perplexed driver and fireman on the loco.

'Go back and sort out our crazy guard,' called the driver, 'he has been showing me alternate red and green flags!'

Feeling rather bemused, I strolled along the platform beside the train (never run, the passengers get worried!) towards the last two coaches of a five-coach train. The guard was leaning out of the window of the brake-van, the fourth vehicle, clutching a green flag.

'What are we waiting for?' he demanded.

'You,' I replied. 'According to your driver you cannot get your act together – first you wave a green, then a red flag, what's going on?'

The fifth and last coach had no corridor, just a number of separate compartments. Suddenly a female head popped out of an open

Before it became a preserved railway company the branch line from Taunton to Minehead, then under the banner of the Great Western Railway and later British Rail, was like many other journeys to a seaside resort, always exciting. It was probably particularly so for entertainers, many of whom were making their professional début in the theatre, and on the last leg of their journey to the little Gaiety Theatre at Minehead (almost within touching distance of the station) to take part in a twenty-week Summer Season at the small but friendly resort. The artistes knew that the residents of the little town of Minehead had been waiting to welcome them through the long winter months. The same sensation would have been felt by the artistes going to Newquay in Cornwall on the last lap from Par Junction, or to Exmouth from Exeter in Devon or to Whitby and Felixstowe on the east coast.

The branch line to Minehead is still there, although it now starts at Bishops Lydiard a couple of miles from Taunton and is owned by the West Somerset Private Railway. It still traverses the same beautiful countryside that it always has done.

Have a look at the restored Great Western Railway signal-box at Bishop's Lydiard before you leave on your journey north. Once you are underway there is a four-mile climb through some lovely country to the award-winning Crowcombe Station. The train now descends very slowly to sea-level still a few miles away.

It's then on to Stogumber, now in sight of the Quantock Hills. This is an unusual station as the station building is on ground-level with the platform opposite. It really is a delightful scene with the station surrounded by a profusion of wild flowers. If you care to break your journey and catch the next train there is a lovely picnic area at Stogumber.

At the next station, Williton, we will have covered half our journey. Williton has the main passing loop on the line and it also has some unusual features. The signal-box is the only remaining one in the country built by the original owners of the line, the Bristol and Exeter Railway. Also inherited from the days of the Bristol and Exeter is the very small but attractive waiting-room with its decorative bargeboards. Adjoining the platform you will see the most amazing garden of box-hedging and every sort of flower imaginable, designed by Charlie Martin who lived in the house adjoining the station. His children and grandchildren have continued the upkeep of this beautiful piece of garden landscaping. In the days of the Great Western Railway and British Rail Charlie, a horticulturalist and market-gardener, used to load up a trolley with produce and arrange for his son Edward to sell it to the passengers who had to wait for another train to pass on the single section of the line.

Doniford Beach Halt is a new station built by the West Somerset Railway in 1986, mainly to serve the nearby holiday complex. Now on to Watchet, the original terminus on the branch from Taunton. Watchet is a very old port and is also remembered before the Second World War as a centre for Territorial Army manoeuvres.

Above: Charlie Martin's wonderful backdrop to Williton Station

Below: award-winning Crowcombe Station

window in that coach.

'Sorry,' she called, 'I heard your conversation. It was all my fault. My little daughter wet her knickers and I have been waving them out of the window to dry!' She then produced and waved said bright-scarlet pants at us to demonstrate!!

If the guard was not amused the driver and fireman certainly were. They 'fell about' the footplate before departing amongst clouds of steam and toots on the whistle!

Walter Harris

NB: *The non-corridor 'suburban' coach has now left the line!*

Further on at Washford Station you will find the headquarters of the Somerset and Dorset Railway Museum Trust. The museum and its surrounding artifacts are well worth a visit. Having previously climbed again to Washford it's now downhill to Blue Anchor Bay and the crossing gates. Blue Anchor also has a very fine museum, housing memorabilia from the Great Western Railway.

We now have Dunster Castle in our sights. Dunster Station itself has an impressive roadside entrance and was built by George Luttrell whose family had lived in the eleventh-century castle since 1376. George Luttrell was the founder of the Minehead to Watchet railway, when the line owned by the West Somerset Railway originally finished at Watchet. Dunster Castle has a magnificent polo lawn used in George Luttrell's day by all the nobility and Indian Princes. Special trains were run to Dunster from Taunton transporting the polo ponies and their grooms.

Now it's dead straight for one and a half miles in to Minehead. The long straight was known as 'High Noon' by the Gaiety Summer Show artistes, who waited for Mum and Dad, or Uncle and Auntie, to arrive to pass a critical eye over their youngsters' ability as entertainers, happy of course in the knowledge that they would be partaking of the sea air and Somerset cream teas during their stay. The 'High Noon' view from Minehead Station to Dunster is quite extraordinary because, just as you did in the past, the first thing you see is a faint plume of smoke before you even see the train. Minehead Station is the largest on the line and

the headquarters of the West Somerset Railway. The platform at which you arrive is a quarter of a mile long and will take a sixteen-coach train. The water tower at the end of the platform came from Pwllheli in North Wales. The camping coaches in the sidings on the south side of the platforms are used as accommodation for working volunteers. The former goods shed on the north side of the platform has been converted to the steam-locomotive depot, which involved among other things building a pit the entire length of it.

The station, opened in July 1874, has been altered several times, but the original buildings still remain and are now used as the company offices and shop. In 1904 a second platform was added, along with track and signal alterations. In 1934 both platforms were doubled in length, the verandah roofing added, and a new signal-box built on the north side. arch 1966 saw the signal-box closed and demolished, with all train movements controlled from Dunster signal-box. In March 1976, when the West Somerset Railway reopened, the signal-box at Dunster, which by now had become redundant, was moved by rail to Minehead and situated on the south side of the line, near the end of the platform. There is plenty to interest the customer at Minehead Station in the company shop, and if you want a snack, hot or cold, there is a buffet car awaiting your convenience, or perhaps you just want to have a gentle walk around this small Somerset holiday resort.

GREAT WESTERN SOCIETY DIDCOT

This is not only a railway centre of restored working locomotives and rolling-stock but also a museum of railway memorabilia of all descriptions. The Society was, believe it or not, the brainchild of four schoolboys who thought it would be a good idea to try to preserve a typical Great Western Railway branch line and perhaps a typical train of that company. From these little acorns grew the magnificent centre that can now be seen at Didcot.

Fundraising and recruiting members for the Society came rather more easily than was expected, and just goes to show what the Great Western Railway holds in people's affections.

Apart from the many engines that would otherwise now be on the scrapheap, the Society has on display an example of Brunel's broad-gauge line put together by a Taunton group of enthusiasts. Other memorabilia in the museum consists of posters, cutlery, china, Great Western Railway jigsaws, uniforms, furniture and many more items. They have a typical GWR country station building which, along with the ticket-office, was rescued from the Newbury to Lambourn line. There are extensive work-

GWR preserved

shops and signalling equipment from other redundant lines and the signal-box from Radstock in Somerset is open to the public at certain times.

The line itself is only a short one, but long enough to show off the great amount of engines and carriages they have.

Meals are served in historic Pullman saloons and they also have the usual shop selling everything a railway buff may want, including their own video 'Didcot, a Celebration', explaining their history and present-day activities. A magazine is distributed worldwide for members of the Society. British Rail Didcot Station adjoins the centre, so there is no excuse for anyone not to hop on a train from Paddington or elsewhere and spend a few hours in the company of the old and trusty Great Western Railway.

Just think that this Society was built on the enthusiasm of four boys who wanted to preserve a piece of our railway heritage. Incidentally, one of those boys is now the Chairman of the Society.

PARTNERSHIP ADDS UP

by David Perry

State industries seldom make friends. Being perceived as more 'Them' than 'Us', it is understandable that in most of us they engender indifference rather than interest, criticism rather than acclaim.

Yet somehow, railways have always been different. Nationalised now for well over forty years, British Rail attracts its fair measure of criticism – some of it justified, much of it rather less so. Yet it is unquestionably true that many people in the UK – perhaps a majority – have a sneaking liking for railways, and there is a wish by common consent to see our railway system prosper. Alter or withdraw a single service, and vitriolic correspondence will be aroused. Close a station – or even propose to rebuild it, and there will be strong protests. Dare to hint at closing an entire line, and the wrath of whole communities will be aroused and there will be questions in the House.

As we approach the new century, our railways still provide to many communities an essential travel service that road cannot easily replace. The railway still puts localities 'on the map'. Stations stand as gateways to the communities they serve; increasingly they are viewed with civic pride.

This change in public attitude has been of critical importance. From a position not so long ago where railways in the UK were regarded as the exclusive responsibility of the state, of concern to the individual only when a train ran late or fares were increased, it is now being recognised that the future of Britain's railways is the direct concern of us all. Local authorities, hitherto concerned only with roads and bus services, are now rapidly realising that they also have responsibilities towards rail. And individual communities are taking a more constructive attitude towards what they are beginning to perceive once more as 'their' railway.

These external changes in attitude have been paralleled by comparable changes in approach within the rail industry, with BR managers at all levels increasingly recognising the value and importance of close co-operative links with the communities in which their business operates.

For an organisation the size and complexity of British Rail, this sort of attitudinal change is far from easy or quick to achieve. As long ago as 1979, it was the then BR Chairman, Sir Peter Parker, who first put forward a collaborative approach to problem-solving – the concept of 'Partnership' – many years before it took on the widespread and common currency of today. Then, as now, its strength lay in its simplicity; a simple recognition of common purpose, a simple agreement to share cost, a simple handshake based on mutual trust, a simple will to cut through 'red tape' and to get something done.

From modest beginnings in the north-west, British Rail's policy of Community Partnership now extends systemwide. It is helping to transform our dreariest inner cities by adding new colour and vitality, it is revitalising the environment of both urban and rural areas, it is reversing the effects of decay and dereliction, it is providing new amenities for the rail-user and enhancing facilities for the disabled and handicapped traveller.

It is bringing together in constructive partnership with BR a wide range of agencies and individuals, in a way that could hardly have been conceived even ten years ago. Local authorities of every political persuasion, enlightened private companies with a concern for the community, civic and voluntary groups with both national and local purpose, agencies of central government concerned with economic revival, training and enterprise generation – all have realised the potential of partnership with BR and have gained from its application.

The range and diversity of this collaborative endeavour is surprisingly wide; partnerships address everything from a simple planting scheme to enhance a station platform, to the macro scale of a major project designed to revitalise a complete rail corridor through the heart of a depressed urban area. The tools of partnership, too, are similarly diverse – 'greening' through planting and landscaping goes hand-in-hand with cleaning, painting and refurbishment, new construction and the creative application of colour and imaginative design.

As you browse through the pages of this book, you will see many practical examples of British Rail partnerships in action – and of the tangible results that are being achieved. You will see communities actively involved in sustaining and improving their local station. You will see individual enthusiasm and commitment working hand-in-hand with the more traditional processes of railway management on a wide range of different projects. You will see, as a consequence, the railway regaining its identity and standing in the community.

Perhaps most of all, you will see effective illustration of the power of collaborative effort towards common goals. In an age concerned – some may say, obsessed – with accountability and a need to balance the books, partnership really does add up.

David Perry is Partnership Manager of the British Rail Community Unit.

THANK YOU FOR TRAVELLING WITH US

I know that somewhere there are other stations which deserve inclusion in this book, but it is not possible to be aware of every instance of picturesque and architectural care and refurbishment. There will be community involvement that I have not heard about, small and large, which is so important to the future well-being of our stations. Perhaps we'll hear about them before a second edition is printed!!

As some of you will realise, the preserved railways I have covered are all standard-gauge lines. That does not mean that the narrower gauge companies are not so popular, in fact most of them provide a very valuable service for tourists and local communities alike. The Festiniog and Talyllyn in Wales, the Romney, Hythe and Dymchurch in Kent and the Isle of Man railways are just a few that have played their part in the revival and interest in the railways in general.

The Surrey British Rail station at Horsley is very gradually being replanted with flowers, tubs and hanging baskets by a local group, and I should think in another six months or so it will complement the new paintwork and general tidying-up that has been carried out there by British Rail.

There have been one or two disappointments as far as I'm concerned and St Ives in Cornwall is one of them. Considering that this area is one of the most popular and well-known tourist resorts in the south-west I feel it deserves more than just a bare wooden platform. Surely something can be done to make it look a little more welcoming. What about the local council putting up some ideas? They needn't be elaborate. A few flower troughs and tubs and perhaps something depicting all the crafts that St Ives is famous for wouldn't go amiss. The town, and presumably the council, benefit from the large amount of people who visit St Ives each year so it wouldn't harm them to put a little effort and a few pounds into *their* station. Nearby Carbis Bay, with its magnificent view has also been neglected and only has a rather nasty corrugated-iron shelter on the platform – UGH!

I also have in mind the Derby to Matlock line which is regularly used by tourists. Needless to say the stations are unmanned but I would have thought this is another great opportunity where the local council and tourist board could join with British Rail to make the stations on the line a little more pleasant for the traveller.

The refurbishment of some mainline stations is quite impressive and deserves a mention. Guildford in Surrey on the London Waterloo to Portsmouth line has been completely redesigned and the interior of the booking-hall is spacious, clean and has an unusual lofty ceiling. There is now ample car-parking space at the station. It would be nice to see a few flowers around the place.

Salisbury in Wiltshire looks good, and the small but tidy entrance has hanging baskets, but although there are also quite a lot of them on the platforms they are too small to make a big impression on this bright station. Penzance was well on the way to its completed refurbishment when I visited it. The huge roof span is being reglazed, and it will certainly be a very pleasing sight on arrival at this last station on one's journey to Cornwall. As there will be a dull-grey finish to the high walls of the interior I do hope the flower displays will be many and varied (my last hint to British Rail). Balcombe on the London Victoria to Brighton line is a small station but it has a couple of well-kept flower-beds and a smallish but neatly trimmed lawn. Stoke on Trent has won prizes in the 'Best Kept Station' competitions and the staff really take good care of it. A local sanitary-ware company supplied and installed the loo, and if you have to visit it while you're there you'll be pleasantly surprised at the cleanliness and design.

The terminus stations of Paddington, Liverpool Street, Charing Cross and Waterloo are undergoing tremendous rebuilding and will look superb when completed, and if you ever have a chance to see the entrances to London's Fenchurch Street and Waterloo after dark you'll enjoy the floodlighting of them I'm sure.

I think the future well-being of our railway stations is generally in good hands, not only in the case of the winners of the Best BR Station Award, Dumfries in 1986 and 1987, Templecombe in 1988, Stoke on Trent in 1989 and Aberdour in 1990, but also at those stations that have come to the notice of other award-winning schemes, large and small, throughout the country.

All these stations deserve the praise of the travelling public and, as far as I'm concerned, without the enthusiasm and hard work I encountered at each of them there certainly would not have been the material available for me to put this book together in the first place.

I found the following guides particularly well presented:

The British Rail Souvenir Guide by Terry Cole
Celebration of the L & S W R by Roger Hardingham
Cranmore Station by Don Sartin
Didcot Junction, A Railway Centre by Laurence Waters
The East Somerset Railway 1858–1972 by Colin C. Maggs
A Guide to the Great Central Railway by James G. Tawse
    and Dennis Wilcock
A Guide to the Watercress Line by Peter Cooper
Isle of Wight Steam Railway by C. P. Whiting, revised
    by I. E. Whitlam
The Lakeside and Haverthwaite Railway, The Companion Guide
The Poppy Line, A Visitor's Guide to the North Norfolk
    Railway by Gordon Perry and Michael Park
Royalty and Empire (The Official Guide to the Windsor
    and Eton Station) by Peter Haylings and Christine Rowley
Steam on the North York Moors by David Joy
The Strawberry Line by David Shepherd
The Worth Valley Experience by Robin Higgins
The Worth Valley Revival by Mark Goodall